# Livestock Survival and Management During Disasters



NIPA® GENX ELECTRONIC RESOURCES & SOLUTIONS P. LTD.
New Delhi-110 034

# Livestock Survival and Management During Disasters


**Mahadevappa D Gouri.** M.V.Sc., Ph.D., PGDBA
Assistant Professor
Department of Livestock Production and Management
Veterinary College, Hebbal, Bangaluru, Karnataka, India

**Y.B. Rajeshwari,** M.V.Sc., Ph.D., FNAP (LPM)
Professor and Head
Department of Livestock Production and Management
Veterinary College, Hebbal, Bangaluru, Karnataka, India

**S.B. Prasanna,** M.V.Sc., Ph.D.
Associate Professor (i/c)
Department of Instructional Livestock Farm Complex
Veterinary College, Hebbal, Bangaluru, Karnataka, India

**Manjunath, Patel.,** M.V.Sc., Ph.D.
Principal Scientist
ICAR National Institute of Veterinary Epidemiology and Disease Informatics
Ramagondanahalli, Yelahanka, Bengaluru-560064
Karnataka, India



NIPA® GENX ELECTRONIC RESOURCES & SOLUTIONS P. LTD.
New Delhi-110 034

nipa®

**NIPA® GENX ELECTRONIC**
**RESOURCES & SOLUTIONS P. LTD.**

101,103, Vikas Surya Plaza, CU Block
L.S.C. Market, Pitam Pura, New Delhi-110 034
Ph : +91 11 27341616, 27341717, 27341718
E-mail: newindiapublishingagency@gmail.com
Web: www.nipabooks.com

***For customer assistance, please contact***
Phone: + 91-11-27 34 17 17
Fax: + 91-11- 27 34 16 16
E-Mail: feedbacks@nipabooks.com



ISBN: 978-81-19215-71-3

This is the Paperback edition of Harback edition



Composed and Designed by NIPA®.

# Preface

This book updates its readers about the methods and management of livestock during disasters.

The book has covered all mad made and natural disasters and their effect on livestock and how they can be managed better for longer survival and help to the humans. Topics on how animals can sense a disaster in advance and what are the common indications given by them and how humans can benefit from it.

Book elucidates the management of feeding, feed resources, production and health so as to make the livestock production economical. It is hoped that the compilation will prove useful for the researchers, planners and policy makers to understand the causes for the loss of productivity and health of livestock in drier regions and help in devising management plans towards sustenance and improvement of production.

**Authors**

# Contents

# 1

# Natural Disasters

### Definition

WHO defines Disaster as "any occurrence, that causes damage, ecological disruption, loss of human life, deterioration of health and health services, on a scale sufficient to warrant an extraordinary response from outside the affected community or area"

Disasters are not totally discrete events. Their possibility of occurrence, time, place and severity of the strike can be reasonably and in some cases accurately predicted by technological and scientific advances. It ha been established there is a definite pattern in their occurrences and hencc we can to some extent reduce the impact of damage itself. This demands the study of disaster management in methodical and orderly approach.

### Disasters are classified in various ways

- Natural disasters and Man made disasters
- Sudden disasters and Slow onset disasters

### Disasters include

- Tornadoes
- Fires
- Hurricanes
- Floods / Sea Surges / Tsunamis
- Snow storms
- Earthquakes
- Landslides
- Severe air pollution (smog)
- Heat waves
- Epidemics
- Building collapse

- Toxicological accidents (e.g. release of hazardous substances)
- Nuclear accidents
- Explosions
- Civil disturbances
- Water contamination and
- Existing or anticipated food shortages

**Haiti Earthquake and Landslides**

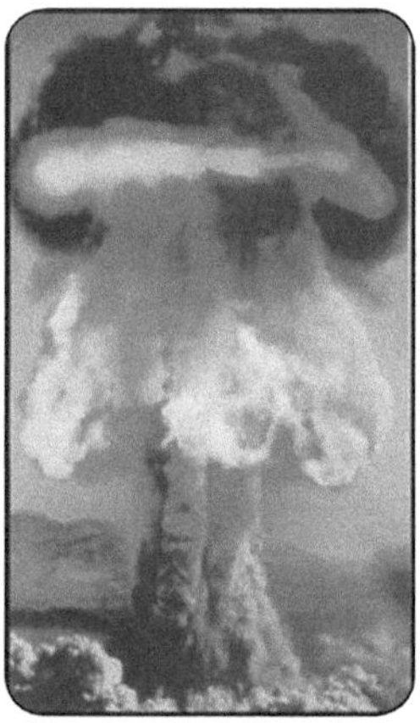

**Nuclear Holocaust** **Destruction By Cyclone**

**India's Natural Disasters Proneness**

On the basis of geographic and climatic considerations, India can be divided into 5 Zones according to its disaster proneness to natural disasters;

1. **Northern mountain region including foot hills:** this region is prone to strong Snow Storms leading to Land slides and strong Cold waves and also is Earthquake prone belt with violent subterranean Volcanic activity.

2. **Indo-gangetic plains:** heavy rains during monsoon make these plains vulnerable to Floods.
3. **Deccan plateau:** a Drought prone area.
4. **The western desert:** a Drought prone area.
5. **Coastal areas:** they are prone to Sea erosion, Cyclones and Tidal waves

**Disaster phase: The phase during which the event of the disaster take place. This phase is characterized by profound damage to the human life. This damage/loss of environment, loss of health or anything else. In this phase, the population is taken by profound shock.**

**Floods**

**India's Disaster Ridden History**

- About 60% of India's land mass is prone to Earthquakes
- Over 40 million Hectares are prone to Floods
- Nearly 3 lakh sq. km are at risk of Cyclones
- The Earthquake in Bhuj killed 14,000 people
- Cyclone in Orissa took away 10,000 lives.
- Between 1990 and 2000 an average of about 3400 people lost their lives annually.
- About 3 crore people were affected by Disasters every year.
- About 17,000 people perished by the Tsunami on 26 December, 2004.

## Vulnerable Populations

A disaster occurring in a deserted area would be considered a natural hazard; but if it occurred in a mega city it would be recognized as a major disaster.

Man made emergencies and another type of emergency that has to do with population vulnerability concerns technological disasters such as those of a Chemical or Radiological or Nuclear in nature. E.g. Bhopal Gas Tragedy.

**Fundamental aspects of disaster management**

1. Disaster Response
2. Disaster Preparedness
3. Disaster Mitigation
4. Disaster Recovery

1. **Response:** The response phase includes the mobilization of the necessary emergency services and first responders in the disaster area. This is likely to include a first wave of core emergency services, such as fire-fighters, police and ambulance crews. When conducted as a military operation, it is termed Disaster Relief Operation (DRO). They may be supported by a number of secondary emergency services, such as specialist rescue teams.
2. **Preparedness:** communication plans with easily understandable terminology and methods. Proper maintenance and training of emergency services, including mass human resources such as community emergency response teams. Development and exercise of emergency population warning methods combined with emergency shelters and evacuation plans. Stockpiling, inventory, and maintain disaster supplies and equipment, develop organizations of trained volunteers among civilian populations.
3. **Mitigation:** Mitigation efforts attempt to prevent hazards from developing into disasters altogether, or to reduce the effects of disasters when they occur. Mitigation is the most cost-efficient method for reducing the impact of hazards, however it is not always suitable. Mitigation does include providing regulations regarding evacuation, sanctions against those who refuse to obey the regulations (such as mandatory evacuations), and communication of potential risks to the public.
4. **Recovery:** The aim of the recovery phase is to restore the affected area to its previous state. Recovery efforts are primarily concerned with actions that involve rebuilding destroyed property, re-employment, and the repair of other essential infrastructure. The assistance for recovery may be provided by national or international agencies and organisations.

**Prevention of Disasters**

- Hurricane/Tornado/ Cyclone warning systems.
- Legislation preventing building in the flood and landslide prone areas
- Requirement of protective cellars/shelters in disaster prone areas
- A Seismic housing code for earthquake-prone area

- Strict procedural code followed to prevent Nuclear, Toxicological and Chemical disasters
- Early warning systems and Disaster preparedness which will help to minimize morbidity, mortality and economic loss

**Surveillance following a disaster evolves in phases**

1. Immediate Assessment
2. Short term assessment
3. Ongoing Surveillance

1. **Immediate assessment:** The object of this phase of surveillance is to obtain as much general information as possible and as quickly as possible.

   **An Arial survey** may be useful in defining the geographical extent of the disaster-stricken area and in observing major damage and destruction.

   **Census data** can be examined to determine how many people previously lived in the disaster-stricken area and thus were at risk.

   **Hospitals, clinics, and morgues**, which were in operation, may be able to obtain numbers of known deaths and injuries.
2. **Short term assessment:** The short-term assessment involves more systematic methods of collecting data and is likely to result in more detailed reliable information on problems, relief resources, and relief information on problems, relief resources and relief activities in progress.
3. **Ongoing surveillance:** Depending on the factors above, short-term assessment may take as little as 5-6 hours or up to 3-4 days. As early as possible, relief priorities should be determined, resources ordered and full scale relief activities initiated.

Once the short-term assessment is complete and appropriate relief is in progress, surveillance becomes an ongoing system.

## Victims and survivors

Almost everyone in the population is affected by a disaster. No one is untouched by it. Those who suffer damage are called victims. The victims may die or live. Those who manage to live are called survivors. These survivors can be classified as:

***Primary survivor*** – One who is exposed to the disaster first-hand and then survives. They are called *'survivor victims'*.

***Secondary survivor*** – One who grieves the loss of primary victims? Example, a mother who lost her child, or a man who lost his friend.

***Third level survivor*** – The rescue and relief personnel. These people are also affected due to the disaster as they are at the site of disaster and undergo almost the same mental trauma as the other victims.

***Fourth level survivor*** – Reporters, Government personnel, traders, etc.

***Fifth level survivor*** – People who read about or see the event in media reports

A relief plan developed during any of the surveillance cycle may include some or all of the following activities:

- Rescue of victims
- Provision of emergency medical care
- Elimination of physical dangers (fire, gas leak etc)
- Evacuation of the population (nuclear and chemical emergencies)
- Provision of preventive and routine medical care to man and animal
- Provision of water
- Provision of food
- Provision of clothing
- Provision of shelter
- Disposal of human waste
- Control of vector born diseases
- Disposal of human and animal bodies
- Disposal of solid waste
- International & national organizations. International Association of Emergency Managers
- Red Cross/Red Crescent
- United Nations
- World Bank
- National Disaster Management Authority of India (NDMAI)
- Emergency Management And Research Institute (EMRI).

## Floods

### Introduction

Floods are the most common and widespread of all natural disasters. India is one of the highly flood prone countries in the world. Around 40 million hectares of land in India is prone to floods as per National Flood Commission report. Floods cause damage to houses, industries, public utilities and property resulting in huge economic losses, apart from loss of lives. Though it is not possible to control the flood disaster totally, by adopting suitable structural and non-structural measures the flood damages can be minimised. For planning any flood management measure latest, reliable, accurate and timely information is required. In this context satellite remote sensing plays an important role.

India has been traditionally vulnerable to natural disasters on account of its unique geo-climatic conditions. Floods, droughts, cyclones, earthquakes and landslides have been a recurrent phenomena. About 60% of the landmass is prone to earthquakes of various intensities; over 40 million hectares is prone to floods; about 8% of the total area is prone to cyclones and 68% of the area is susceptible to drought. In the decade 1990-2000, an average of about 4344 people lost their lives and about 30 million people were affected by disasters every year. The loss in terms of private, community and public assets has been astronomical.

At the global level, there has been considerable concern over natural disasters. Even as substantial scientific and material progress is made, the loss of lives and property due to disasters has not decreased. In fact, the human toll and economic losses have mounted. It was in this background that the United Nations

General Assembly, in 1989, declared the decade 1990–2000 as the International Decade for Natural Disaster Reduction with the objective to reduce loss of lives and property and restrict socio-economic damage through concerted international action, specially in developing countries.

The super cyclone in Orissa in October, 1999 and the Bhuj earthquake in Gujarat in January, 2001 underscored the need to adopt a multi dimensional endeavour involving diverse scientific, engineering, financial and social processes; the need to adopt multi disciplinary and multi sectoral approach and incorporation of risk reduction in the developmental plans and strategies.

Over the past couple of years, the Government of India have brought about a paradigm shift in the approach to disaster management. The new approach proceeds from the conviction that development cannot be sustainable unless disaster mitigation is built into the development process. Another corner stone of the approach is that mitigation has to be multi-disciplinary spanning across all sectors of development. The new policy also emanates from the belief that investments in mitigation are much more cost effective than expenditure on relief and rehabilitation.

Disaster management occupies an important place in this country's policy framework as it is the poor and the under-privileged who are worst affected on account of calamities/disasters. The steps being taken by the Government emanate from the approach outlined above. The approach has been translated into a National Disaster Framework covering institutional mechanisms, disaster prevention strategy, early warning system, disaster mitigation, preparedness and response and human resource development. The expected inputs, areas of intervention and agencies to be involved at the National, State and district levels have been dentified and listed in the roadmap. This roadmap has been shared with all the State Governments and Union Territory Administrations. Ministries and Departments of Government of India, and the State Governments/UT Administrations have been advised to develop their respective roadmaps taking the national roadmap as a broad guideline. There is, therefore, now a common strategy underpinning the action being taken by all the participating organisations/stakeholders.

The changed approach is being put into effect through:

(a) Institutional changes
(b) Enunciation of policy
(c) Legal and techno-legal framework
(d) Mainstreaming Mitigation into Development process
(e) Funding mechanism
(f) Specific schemes addressing mitigation
(g) Preparedness measures
(h) Capacity building
(i) Human Resource Development and, above all, community participation.

## Rescue and Evacuation

Evacuation is a pre-emptive move to protect life and property, where as rescue is a post-disaster phenomenon of helping people to move from areas that have been hit by disaster to a safer place. However, the situation of evacuation and rescue comes along with numerous unanswered queries in mind. Very often, due to lack of information or in haste, living during evacuation and rescue becomes difficult and painful. However, during such the situations, following precautionary norms should be kept in mind.

## Preparing for a Flood

Here are some basic steps to take to prepare for the flood:

- Contact the local geologist or town planning department or meteorology department to find out if your home is located in a flash-flood-prone area or landslide-prone area.
- Learn about your community's emergency plans, warning signals, evacuation routes, and locations of emergency shelters.
- Plan and practice a flood evacuation route with your family. Ask an out-of-state relative or friend to be the "family contact" in case your family is separated during a flood. Make sure everyone in your family knows the name, address, and phone number of this contact person.
- Post emergency phone numbers at every phone.
- Inform local authorities about any special needs, i.e., elderly or bedridden people, or anyone with a disability.
- Identify potential home hazards and know how to secure or protect them before the flood strikes. Be prepared to turn off electrical power when there is standing water, fallen power lines etc. Turn off gas and water supplies before you evacuate. Secure structurally unstable building materials.
- Buy a fire extinguisher and make sure your family knows where it is and how to use it.
- Buy and install sump pumps with back-up power.
- Have a licensed electrician to raise electric components (switches, sockets, circuit breakers and wiring) at least 12" above your home's projected flood elevation.
- For drains, toilets, and other sewer connections, install backflow valves or plugs to prevent floodwaters from entering.
- Anchor fuel tanks which can contaminate your basement if torn free. An unanchored tank outside can be swept downstream and damage other houses.

If you are under a flood watch or warning:

- Gather the emergency supplies you previously stocked in your home and stay tuned to local radio or television station for updates.
- Turn off all utilities at the main power switch and close the main gas valve if evacuation appears necessary.
- Have your immunization records handy or be aware of your last tetanus shot, in case you should receive a puncture wound or a wound becomes contaminated during or after the flood.

- Fill bathtubs, sinks and plastic soda bottles with clean water. Sanitize the sinks and tubs first by using bleach. Rinse and fill with clean water.
- Bring outdoor possessions, such as lawn furniture, grills and trash cans inside or tie them down securely.

**Emergency Supplies You Will Need**

You should stock your home with supplies that may be needed during the emergency period. At a minimum, these supplies should include:

- Several clean containers for water, large enough for a 3-5 day supply of water (about five gallons for each person).
- A 3-5 day supply of non-perishable food and a non-electric can opener.
- A first aid kit and manual and prescription medicines and special medical needs.
- A battery-powered radio, flashlights, and extra batteries.
- Sleeping bags or extra blankets.
- Water-purifying supplies, such as chlorine or iodine tablets or unscented, ordinary household chlorine bleach.
- Baby food and/or prepared formula, diapers, and other baby supplies.
- Disposable cleaning cloths, such as "baby wipes" for the whole family to use in case bathing facilities are not available.
- Personal hygiene supplies, such as soap, toothpaste, sanitary napkins, etc.
- An emergency kit for your car with food, flares, booster cables, maps, tools, a first aid kit, fire extinguisher, sleeping bags, etc.
- Rubber boots, sturdy shoes, and waterproof gloves.
- Insect repellent containing DEET, screens, or long-sleeved and long-legged clothing for protection from mosquitoes which may gather in pooled water remaining after the flood.

**Preparing to Evacuate**

Expect the need to evacuate and prepare for it. When a flood watch is issued, you should:

- Fill your vehicle's gas tank and make sure the emergency kit for your car is ready.
- If no vehicle is available, make arrangements with friends or family for transportation.

- Fill your clean water containers.
- Review your emergency plans and supplies, checking to see if any items are missing.
- Tune in the radio or television for weather updates.
- Listen for disaster sirens and warning signals.
- Put livestock and family pets in a safe area. Due to food and sanitation requirements, emergency shelters cannot accept animals.
- Adjust the thermostat on refrigerators and freezers to the coolest possible temperature.

### If You Are Ordered to Evacuate

You should never ignore an evacuation order. Authorities will direct you to leave if you are in a low-lying area, or within the greatest potential path of the rising waters. If a flood warning is issued for your area or you are directed by authorities to evacuate the area, follow the below mentioned checklists:

- Take only essential items with you.
- If you have time, turn off the gas, electricity, and water.
- Disconnect appliances to prevent electrical shock when power is restored.
- Follow the designated evacuation routes and expect heavy traffic.
- Do not attempt to drive or walk across creeks or flooded roads.

### If You Are Ordered NOT to Evacuate

To get through the storm in the safest possible manner:

- Monitor the radio or television for weather updates.
- Prepare to evacuate to a shelter or to a neighbour's home if your home is damaged, or if you are instructed to do so by emergency personnel

### Safety and Security

Any natural calamities espouse itself with serious devastation to transportation, communication channel, supply of electricity etc. Hence, in the immediate aftermath of any calamity, the surrounding environment becomes dangerous and unsafe due to it's exposure to toxic and harmful objects. This becomes more important for children as they are usually overlooked by the parents during the calamity or in the immediate aftermath of it.

## Risk Management and Flood Plain Delineation

A change to proactive management of natural disasters requires an identification of the risk, the development of strategies to reduce that risk, and the creation of policies and programmes to put these strategies into effect. Risk management is a fundamental activity geared to the evaluation of schemes for reducing but not necessarily eliminating the overall risk, as in many cases risk cannot be entirely eliminated. Figure 8 provides a schematic of the steps associated with risk assessment and management. It includes assessing the potential for a hazard to occur and a vulnerability analysis to provide an understanding of the consequences should an event of a certain magnitude and frequency occur. Based on this initial work, various mitigation measures can be evaluated to assess their ability for reducing risk exposure. Based on a thorough risk assessment, disaster management plans and specific mitigation measures can be identified. Efforts would then be undertaken to implement the selected mitigation measures. For flooding events, there is a need to calculate the probability or likelihood that an extreme event will occur and to establish and estimate the social, economic and environmental implications should the event occur under existing conditions. Maps of the flood-prone areas should be prepared and detailed impacts outlined. A participatory process should be invoked, leading to the development of an acceptable level of risk. Measures can be evaluated and implemented to meet this level. This overall process assists the community in better understanding the various actions that can increase or decrease risk exposure, and can lead to greater community participation in the developed solutions to the flooding problem.

## Preparedness and response plans

Detailed response plans need to be prepared in advance and reviewed with all of the key agencies and players. There is no one "common" response plan as the linkages will be different in each case. The response to a toxic chemical spill is very different from the response to a major fire or flood. Not only must the plan be in writing and available to hose that will be responding, but also it must be continually reviewed and updated. Some of the key pieces of information are: which agency and individuals have the specific responsibility; whom to contact for expert advice; and where to go for information on backup communication systems. This information is constantly changing and needs to be verified periodically and tested in exercises. Multiple contact points need to be established as the emergency may occur on a weekend, holiday, or after regular business hours. Mechanisms for coordination must be included in the plan, including the structure of response committees, where they will meet and sources of resource information available to them. Often this takes the form of something equivalent to a "war room" where maps, plans, other material and support staff are available immediately.

### Inventory of resources

A key component of any emergency preparedness plan is an inventory of resources that can be accessed. In the case of flooding this could include items such as emergency vehicles, buses and trucks, earthmoving equipment, pumps, plastic, plywood, emergency generators, supplies of gravel and sand, sandbags, and mobile communications equipment. The inventory should also include access to expertise such as surveyors, levee or slope stability experts, forecasting specialists, the media and community leaders. Emergency shelters should be designated in advance, their individual capacity defined and plans made for obtaining sufficient supplies of water, food, medicine and medical/social assistance. If local resources are not sufficient, then the availability circle must be expanded to include adjacent communities, the provincial/state and national government levels.

### Triggering emergency action

Advance warning is the key to effective response. It is possible to set up a series of warnings in advance of an actual extreme storm event that can be used as alerts. This could start with long-term climatologic forecasts or more immediate hurricane forecasts that identify potential danger. For specific basins an alert could be issued based on antecedent precipitation and rainfall intensity data in advance of an actual flood forecast. A more detailed forecast would then be issued when all of the data and information required to make a flood forecast became available.

The emergency response to such alerts is very site-specific and should be included in the plan. If, for example, emergency actions such as temporary levees are necessary, then the work could begin based on an alert rather than the specific forecast. The same may hold for emergency evacuation. The response to an extreme flood forecast should be immediate, and with no uncertainty as to what actions and activities should be taken. The public expects governments to act quickly and in a professional manner under such circumstances. Community leaders should be visible, informed and active right from the start.

### Training and response exercises

Emergency response teams need to be well trained in advance and their skills onstantly upgraded. Once the disaster strikes, it is too late to train or try to find missing expertise. Trained staff should know their responsibilities, have immediate access to response plans and other critical information, and already have built a working relationship with colleagues in other organizations. The only meaningful way to test response plans is to carry out periodic emergency exercises. These exercises are meant to simulate real emergency situations and test all aspects of the plan. Costs are significant, but have real payback in an actual emergency. Often critical gaps are identified and appropriate backup strategies developed as part of the exercise.

**Advance preparation**

Assuming that there is advance warning of a major storm event, a number of steps can be taken to increase readiness. Such steps include: construction of temporary flood protection works; placing emergency response teams on high alert; distribution of critical materials such as stockpiled sandbags to targeted locations; and preparation of emergency shelters and hospitals prepared for occupation. The population at risk can be informed of what is expected of them in the actuality of an extreme event. As the event becomes more certain, actions such as evacuation of people, goods and machinery can begin. Even if the event is not as extreme as predicted, these preparations help test emergency response plans and inform the public as to the nature of natural hazards. Media and public information sessions help set the stage as well. The media are key players in the link between public officials and the public. It helps if they are familiar with the terminology used in warnings and forecasts and know whom to contact for more detailed information during an actual flood event.

**After the flood event**

The emergency response does not end with the event, but continues through cleanup and resettlement stages. People will want to know what assistance will be made available, who is responsible, and how to go about seeking that assistance. Senior levels of government should develop clearly defined response policies and programmes in advance. In the absence of such policies, the response is often ad hoc, politically and emotionally motivated, and sets precedents that are not wise in the longer run. Often the response is incomplete in that the obvious and immediate requirements are addressed, but fundamental changes in thinking and sustainable strategies are ignored. After a major flood it is beneficial to conduct an assessment of the causes and effects of the flood and to make recommendations that would improve preparedness for the next event and reduce future flood losses. Such an assessment can also lead to improvements in flood plain management policies. The long-term economic and social implications of flooding become evident in the post-disaster period. Governments need to demonstrate leadership and sometimes take bold steps to restore employment, address social issues and move the economy in a new direction. In that sense, natural disasters can be a positive motivator for change.

## Management of Livestock During Drought

Livestock plays a crucial role, contributing through milk, meat, wool and their products. Materialization of optimum utilization of feed and fodder resources to combat scarcity, needs practical strategies through planner's to enhance livestock productivity in India and other developing countries. Livestock productivity is becoming a major consideration for many developing programs. According to FAO estimate of 2008,the country had 185.181 million cattle, 97.9 million buffaloes, 124.4 million goats, 61.42 million sheep, 13.5 million swine and 489 million poultry. Population figures indicate that Indian cattle, buffalo, sheep, goat contribute 16, 54 , 5 and 21%, respectively of world population. Put together these livestock contribute 1830 billion rupees to GNP, which in turn is 32% of 27% contributed by agriculture.

Natural calamities are chronic problems of India which adversely affect the health and production of farm animals and poultry due to occurrence of feed deficit. The shortage of livestock feeding is caused by floods and droughts and there is no single year in the Indian history ' in which the floods have not occurred in one part of the country and the droughts in the other. The scarcity of animal feed caused by floods is of a temporary nature. During the droughts, however severe shortage of animal feed especially roughages is encountered. This has an adverse effect on feed resources as dried roughages alone account for over 50–80 per cent of supply of dry matter and TDN required for ruminants' viz., sheep, cattle and goats. Failure of monsoon is the main factor responsible for droughts in Asia. While co-efficient of variation in monsoon rainfall for the Indian subcontinent is only 10 per cent, the same for Gujarat, Maharashtra, Karnataka, Andhra Pradesh and Rajasthan is over 35 per cent. In parts of Rajasthan, Gujarat, Saurashtra and some districts of the Deccan Plateau it ranges from 50–100 per cent. Certain areas are, therefore, more prone for fodder scarcity than others. Incidentally, these areas make a major contribution towards production of oilseeds and coarse grains. The shortage of these crops aggravates the supply of oil cakes and straws. Perennial irrigation system has been developed in such areas through construction of dams and canals. However, redeeming feature in supply of livestock feed is that the commercial crops continue to be cultivated in selected pockets with ensured irrigation even in the worst drought affected zones.

The use of products of such commercial crops, drought resistant vegetations, in combination with NPN source of protein and by-products of molasses as source of energy could be used for meeting the immediate nutritional requirements under conditions of scarcity. Certain varieties of tree leaves and cakes of inedible oilseeds could be used to meet the essential requirements of intact protein in ruminants. This strategy was successfully applied in the State of Maharashtra in India during droughts of 1972-73. The cattle relief camps were set up around the sugarcane factories located in the drought affected zones. Large scale feeding of bagasse, molasses in combination with urea and mineral supplements was adopted. The feed formulations developed through experimentation were tried on large population of cattle without any detrimental effects.

**Definition:** Drought is defined as the extended period of deficient rainfall relative to the average for a region.

### Causes of Drought

- Inadequacy of rainfall, or lack of irrigation facilities.
- Under-exploitation or deficient availability for meeting the normal crop requirements in the context of the agro-climatic conditions prevailing in any particular area.

### Types of Drought

Drought proceeds in sequential manner. Its impacts are spread across different domains as listed below.

- **Meteorological drought:** It is simple absence/deficit of rainfall from the normal. It is the least severe form of drought and is often identified by sunny days and hot weather.
- **Hydrological drought**: often it is reduction of natural stream flows or groundwater levels, plus stored water supplies.
- **Agricultural drought:** It occurs when moisture level in soils is insufficient to maintain average crop yields. At extreme it can lead to a famine( which is a prolonged shortage of food in a restricted region) causing widespread disease and death from starvation.

### Effects of Drought

- Reduced pregnancy rates.
- Lower milk production which lowers weaning weights.
- Loss of body condition of the animal.
- widespread crop failure, unreplenished ground water resources, depletion in lakes/reservoirs, shortage of drinking water and reduced fodder availability.

### Effects on Wildlife

- Alligators fare reasonably well because of the temporary concentration of prey items into remaining water, but there may be increased cannibalism.
- Under prolonged drought, they may be forced to move in search of water. Traveling over dry land can cause increased mortality from motor vehicles as well as dehydration. And smaller alligators may fall prey to predators.
- Birds are generally unaffected by local drought as they can move easily to find water.
- Prolonged drought could have significant impacts on the hatchlings and juvenile tortoises.
- Native reptiles and amphibians are adapted to periodic droughts and occasional wildfires. Droughts and fires can cause elevated mortality of reptiles and amphibians.
- Four main components to drought response mechanisms have been identified:
- **Drought alert**: consensus must be reached at the community, district and national levels with regard to drought indicators and on categorizations of drought conditions (e.g. mild, moderate, and severe).
- **Response processes**: for each category of drought, agreement should be reached on specific, concrete action to be taken and the levels at which the tasks will be performed (i.e. district, national or local). The roles and responsibilities of the different stakeholders should be clearly defined.
- **Co-ordination**: effective coordination among all the different actors in drought interventions is of critical importance.
- **Listening to local communities**: local people are often overlooked when contingency plans for droughts are drawn up. Herders and farmers may often know the most efficient means of aiding drought responses in their communities and thus help to establish effective and sustainable measures.

## Elephant Died in Kenya Due to Drought

Droughts differ from other natural hazards in several important ways:

- Slow-onset, creeping phenomenon that makes it difficult to determine the onset and end of the event;
- Duration may range from months to years;
- No universal definition;
- No single indicator or index can identify precisely the onset and severity of the event;
- Impacts are generally non-structural and difficult to quantify;
- Spatial extent is usually much greater than for other natural hazards, making assessment and response actions difficult, since impacts are spread over larger geographical areas;
- By their potentially long duration, the core area or epicenter will change over time, reinforcing the need for continuous monitoring of climate and water supply indicators.
- Impacts are cumulative and the effects magnify when events continue from one season or year to the next.

  All these points make drought management much difficult.

## Management

The strategy can be subdivided into three basic categories:

1. Livestock inventory
2. Efficient use of existing forage resources
3. Developing alternative forage supplies.

- Support for herder mobility and access to productive pastures.
- Protect animals from the effects of the drought by feeding or relocating them.
- Adequate storage and protection of food and water available.
- Identifying animals so they can easily be reunited with their owners.
- Ensure the methods for removing animals safely from the drought affected areas.
- Strengthen and secure animal shelters.
- Carry regular vaccination programmes to protect animals from diseases during drought stress.

**Use existing forage resources efficiently**

- Meanwhile, prevent cattle herders illegally driving their animals deep into parks and reserves in search of water and grazing land.
- Make every effort to reduce feed wastage.
- Feed the highest quality feeds to animals having highest nutrient requirements.
- Feed the lowest quality feeds to cows in the middle stage of pregnancy.
- Save the better quality feeds for those periods just before and after calving.
- Consider ammoniating crop residues such as wheat and barley straw to improve digestibility and intake.
- Provide emergency veterinary care.
- Rehabilitation- Aim to get living conditions back to normal – or improve them – for all affected animals.
- Move cattle to a remote pasture or to rented pastures outside the drought area. Follow rotational grazing (increases pasture efficiency).
- Cull cows that are open, old and low producers. This will provide more feed for younger and more productive cows.
- Culling priorities should start with replacement heifer's first, open cows second, old cows third, and then low producers.
- Either sells calves at younger ages or weans and feed them separately from cows.
- If early weaning is not an option, then creep feeding is an excellent alternative.
- Culling combined with early weaning will cut the feed needed for cows by at least half.
- Provide supplemental feed (e.g. purchased forage, calf creep feed)
- Hay is the most often used option. But grains and by-product feeds are often cheaper per unit of energy than hay.
- Grain should be gradually introduced over a ten-day period - longer for wheat.
- Adequate supply of fresh water, particularly when stocks are being fed concentrates.
- It is important to group cows by nutrient needs, such as production status, age, and body condition, which can avoid over or under feeding a particular group, thus reducing supplemental feed costs.

**Developing alternative forage supplies.**

The following supplements can be considered during drought:

1. *Range cubes* - They require no feed troughs, are convenient, but expensive
2. *Liquid Supplements, molasses blocks, and protein blocks* - These are convenient, but expensive.
3. *Grain, by-products* - These feeds are equal in energy to corn when fed as a supplement to a forage-based diet.
4. *Self-Fed Supplements* - Rations containing a protein supplement with salt can provide 2.5–3.5 pounds of supplement per cow per day when fed fair quality hay free-choice or limited grazing.

- Available crop residues such as small grain straws and other byproducts of crop production represent important methods of stretching tight feed supplies during drought.
- Take advantage of weedy growth in crop residues and pasture patches as well as roadsides, woodlots, etc. as permitted.
- Avoid overgrazing rangeland, otherwise recovery following drought will be slow and production depressed for an extended time.
- Buy hay early and store hay while it is inexpensive.
- Adoption of low cost and efficient irrigation practices of sprinkler and drip irrigation which additionally saves 40 % of the water available for irrigation.
- Emphasis on less water consuming crops suitable to local conditions.
- Pre-drought planning
- Optimize the use of soils and forage species.
- Grow high yielding hybrid variety of crops.
- Harvest rain water.
- Develop a hay storage plan.
- Develop a relocation plan for the base herd to an area not affected by drought.
- After the drought
- Rest pastures until the target grazing height is achieved.
- Graze pastures to target stubble height.
- Use N fertilizer to increase production.
- Reseed legumes and grasses as needed.
- Use annual forages during pasture renovation.

### Precautions

- The use of salt to limit supplement intake increase water intake by 50 to 75 percent. Water must not be limited in any way, or salt toxicity may result.
- Over-consumption of **urea**-containing supplements by cattle on forage scarce ranges may result in ammonia toxicity.
- Hay cut under moisture stress conditions, especially grain type hays, may contain high levels of nitrate.
- Prussic acid or **c**yanide poisoning can also be a problem in grazing drought-stunted plants such as sorghum, sorghum hybrids, and Sudan grass. So forage for hay is allowed to sun cure thoroughly for three to five days.
- Cattle grazing short pasture are more likely to consume poisonous plants.
- Rumen impaction may result by inadequate protein and low quality/high fiber forage as in drought. Inadequate water will aggravate the problem.
- Hardware disease—Hay harvested from vacant city lots, roadsides, etc., may contain nails, wire, or foreign objects that can pierce the rumen wall resulting in death of the animal.

## Cyclones

### Definition

Cyclones are like giant whirlwinds of air and dense cloud spiraling at over 120 km/h around a central 'eye' of extreme low pressure

- ***Frequency*** **-** Cyclones occur frequently in the southern hemisphere, with an average of ten per year being tracked by the Bureau of Meteorology in the Australian region alone. Of these, six may be expected to cross the Australian coast each year. Cyclones further out in the Indian and Pacific Oceans are monitored in case they threaten Australian islands or nearby countries.
- ***Severity Categories*** **-** These range from '1' for weak cyclones (strongest wind gusts less than 125 km/h), through '2' (125-169 km/h), '3' (170-224 km/h), '4' (225-279 km/h), to '5' for the most severe cyclones (wind gusts more than 280 km/h).
- ***Effects*** **-** Cyclones approach from the sea bringing with them torrential rains, extreme winds and sometimes storm surges (explained later). Damage caused by each cyclone varies widely depending on its path, but can include buildings, crops and boats at sea. Most deaths from cyclones occur as a result of drownings (both at sea and during floods), collapsed buildings, or debris which become lethal projectiles carried along by the extreme winds.

- ***Cyclone Mahina*** - This terrible storm in March 1899, which was accompanied by a storm surge of over 10 metres, caused by far the highest death toll of any cyclone before or since, claiming over 400 lives as it completely destroyed a pearling fleet at Bathurst Bay near Cape Melville, Queensland. Deaths included the crews of 100 vessels and an estimated 100 local aborigines.

### The Birth and Anatomy of cyclone

The 'life-cycle' of the average tropical cyclone (or hurricane/typhoon) is about seven days but can extend to over three weeks. They form in the atmosphere over warm ocean areas with at least 26°C water temperature (mainly in latitudes 5° to 20° north or south) although their exact trigger-mechanism is not fully understood. If conditions are right, an ordinary tropical depression, or 'low' can develop into a tropical cyclone.

In the southern hemisphere, in a 'low', the winds spiral in a clockwise direction towards its centre, where they rise and spill over in an outward flow at high altitude. Summer heat beating on the warm ocean evaporates water, creating a deep layer of moist air. The uplift of this moist air in the centre of a 'low' cools it, causing the intense rain characteristic of tropical cyclones. Higher in the upper levels the rising air spirals outward, removing air faster than it flows in, resulting in a fall in barometric pressure.

### The Central 'Eye'

Cyclones vary greatly in character but the one feature they all have in common is a virtually calm centre with clear sky. This centre, or 'eye' is generally about 16–30 km across, but even this can range from 10–100 km. Around this eye are bands of heavy cloud, associated with the moist air which spirals in towards the centre of the cyclone. These clouds, known as the 'eye wall', may be 15 km high and mark the ring of strongest winds and heaviest rainfall

### Cyclone Behaviour and Warning Time

Research shows that tropical cyclones in the Australian region have more erratic tracks than those in other parts of the world. Cyclones may exist for a few days, to over three weeks! They may move forward, double-back, stay motionless for periods, or move in circles, and therefore need to be tracked carefully by weather observers (see map below). If they reach land, the friction of the earth and the loss of sustaining heat energy from the ocean, cause cyclones to 'fill' and drop most of their rain. As cyclones move forward at only 15–25 km/h, there is usually sufficient warning time for people to prepare for their onset.

### Lethal Energy

Tropical cyclones are the greatest storms on earth, releasing in one day as much condensation heat energy as up to four hundred, 20 megaton atomic bombs. Every cyclone is dangerous and must be regarded as a real threat until the danger has clearly passed. Where tropical cyclones are concerned, because of their erratic paths, there is no such thing as a 'false-alarm' - the community which has been by-passed by a cyclone knows it has been lucky **this time**

### Beware the 'Eye'

It is important for people in cyclone areas to be aware that if the 'eye' of the cyclone passes over them, there will be a sudden lull in wind and clearing of skies, which may last anywhere from a few minutes to an hour or two. Then the other side of the cyclone will strike and the winds will resume with equal strength, but blowing from the **opposite direction**. It is, therefore, most important that people should remain in shelter during and after the passing of the 'eye'

### Storm Surge

One other effect of a cyclone is that it can produce a storm surge (or tide). A storm surge may be caused by cyclonic winds blowing across the water and a fall in atmospheric pressure. The lower pressure at the eye of the cyclone actually allows a sea-level rise in, and close to, that centre. This raised dome of water is usually 60-80 km across and 2 to 5 metres higher than normal sea-level. As a cyclone nears the coast, low-lying areas may suffer flooding because strong on-shore winds have displaced the storm surge ahead of the cyclone's centre.

The amount of flooding that occurs depends very much on the height of the tide when the cyclone crosses the coast. If the tide is fairly low, flooding may not occur. The diagram shows how sea-level can be affected by surrounding wind and air pressure as the cyclone's centre crosses the coast.

### Cyclone Survival and Property Protection

In cyclone-prone areas of Australia, strict building codes exist for all new constructions. In some areas public cyclone shelters are provided in strong buildings for people who live or work in sub-standard buildings. A cyclone warning system is provided by the Bureau of Meteorology, and State/Territory Emergency Services run preparedness campaigns to support community emergency plans. If you live in a cyclone-prone area you should heed this advice:

**Before the Cyclone Season**

- Know your community cyclone plan, and how the cyclone warning system works.
- Have a portable radio and torch with spare batteries.
- Check your house is in good condition, particularly the roof, and trim tree branches clear of your house. Clear property of loose items likely to cause damage in high winds.
- In case of a storm surge warning, identify your nearest safe, high area in advance.
- Create an emergency kit of tinned food, water containers, emergency lighting, first aid kit, medicines, tape and plastic bags.

**Upon a Cyclone Warning**

- Listen to your local radio or TV for further warnings.
- Board or tape windows, store loose articles inside.
- Lock up pets, fill water containers, fuel car and place under cover.
- Check your emergency kit and put spare clothing and shoes in plastic bags.

**On Warning of a Local Evacuation**

- Switch off electricity, gas, etc and lock your house upon leaving.
- Don't forget your emergency kit. Follow instructions from emergency personnel.

**When the Cyclone Strikes**

- Stay inside and shelter in strongest part of the house (eg bathroom or cellar).
- Protect yourself with mattress, blankets and anchor yourself to a strong fixture (such as water pipes) or get under a strong table.
- Beware the calm 'eye'. Remain indoors until advised that the cyclone has passed.

**After the Cyclone**

- Don't go outside until advised officially that the cyclone has passed.
- Listen to your radio for further information and advice.
- If you had to evacuate, don't go home until advised. Use recommended routes.

- Beware of fallen power lines, damaged buildings, trees and flooded watercourses.

## Earthquake-A Natural Disaster

**An Earthquake**: It is a Natural Disaster, an undesirable occurrence resulting from forces that are likely outside human control. Earthquake is one among them, and the most unpredictable and highly destructive of all the natural disasters. More than 80% of natural disasters are due to earthquakes. Earthquakes have proved to be most devastating and their area of influence is also large.

### Cause

- The tectonic plates in the earth crust are moving, up to a few centimeters per year, and some of them are colliding. When this happens stress is accumulated. Sometimes this stress release is so high that it produces a friction in the plates and this, in essence, is the earthquake
- Most vulnerable states are Jammu and Kashmir, Himachal Pradesh,Uttarakhand, Sikkim, West Bengal, Gujarat and Maharashtra.
- More than 1,200 earthquakes have occurred in India till now.
- Zone 1- very low damage risk zone
- Zone 2- low damage risk zone
- Zone 3- moderate damage risk zone
- Zone 4- high damage risk zone
- Zone 5- very high damage risk zone

### Socio-Environmental Consequences

- Earthquakes have devastating effects which differ in magnitude depending upon it's scale, it is more worrying when it strikes densely populated area.
- It not only damages the infrastructure, transport, developmental activities but also communication network, and robs the population of their settlements, land, house and animals

### Effects of Earthquakes

**1. On land**

- Causes fissures/cracks in settlements,
- Landslides,

- Avalanches, Mudslides,
- Causes cracks in the upper layers of the
- Earth crust through which water and volatile materials gush out and flood the neighboring areas,
- Also causes obstruction in the flow of rivers and channels resulting in floods and other calamities in surrounding areas.

**2. On man made settlements**

- Over turning of buildings,
- Collapse of bridges, dams,
- Cracks in the building, monuments.

**3. In water**

- Big waves in sea Tsunami,
- Hydro dynamic pressures affecting coastal life.

**How is Earthquake Measured?**

**Depending on the magnitude:** The amount of energy released during an earthquake, which is computed from the amplitude of the seismic waves. A magnitude of 7.0 on the Richter scale indicates an extremely strong earthquake. Each whole number on the scale represents an increase of about 30 times more energy released than the previous whole number represents.

Therefore, an earthquake measuring 6.0 is about 30 times more powerful than one measuring 5.0.

**Precautionary measures: Providing timely relief in case of earthquake affected areas is very difficult task as most of transport and communication links are destroyed in most of the cases.**

Hence it is better if we prepare before hand in vulnerable areas;

1. First step: Establishing earthquake monitoring centers (Seismological centers) for regular monitoring & fast dissemination of information among people. Use of GPS can be of great help.
2. Preparing vulnerability maps and educating people of those areas about ways and steps of helping themselves and their livestock during earthquake.
3. Modifying the house types & building designs in vulnerable areas, such as discouraging high rise buildings, large industrial establishments, and suggest the use of earthquake resistant design & light materials in construction of human & livestock dwellings.

4. Have Disaster Supplies on Hand-
    - Educate the people,
    - Reducing hazards throughout the home, workplace like placing heavy materials, large glass stuff on roof, can greatly reduce risk of injury or death following the earthquake ,
        - First aid kit and manual,
        - Emergency food and water,
        - Essential medicines,
    - Locate emergency communication link and try to contact local rescue org / management.
    - Livestock/animals should not be housed in closed housing system. Any warning / information regarding, earthquake if received before hand, make sure all the livestock can be evacuated and transported to safe place by possible transport means available.
    - Livestock can be fed with non-conventional feeds like tree leaves, shrubs etc. during such disaster.
5. Use of helicopters, Air force to rescue people and animals from earthquake affected areas.

**What to do after an Earthquake?**

1. Expect aftershocks and be careful,
2. Stay away from damaged areas,
3. Lookout for possible floods and take appropriate measures,
4. Check electrical damage and buildings cracked in the vicinity and avoid coming in contact with it.
5. Help injured and trapped humans
6. Immediately try contacting the rescue teams.

**Haiti Earthquake 2010**

It's a Creole and French speaking Caribbean country. It's the poorest country in the western hemisphere and is ranked 149$^{th}$ of 182 countries on the HDI.

It's considered as economically vulnerable by FAO and its not strange to natural disasters.

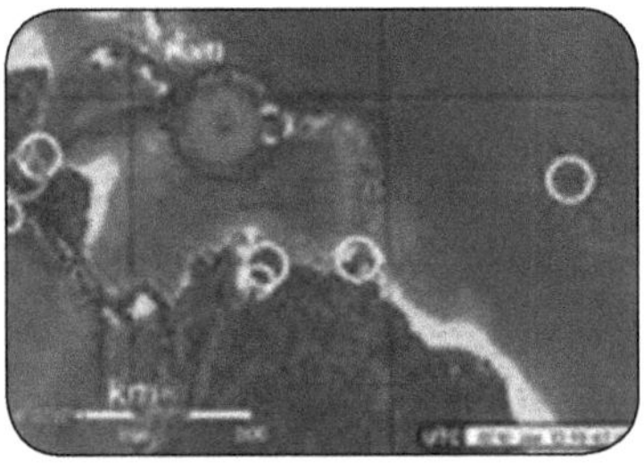

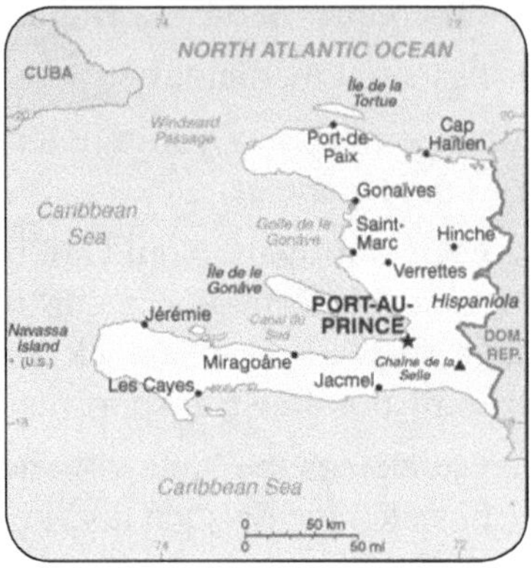


Date: 12th January 2010

Magnitude: 7 Mw

Depth: 13 km

Casualties: 2,30,000 confirmed deaths, 3,00,000 injuries, and 10,00000 homeless

By 14th of January a thousand bodies had been placed on the streets and pavements.

Post au prince's morgues were quickly overwhelmed; tens of thousands of bodies were buried in mass graves

**Rescue and relief efforts**

- Over the first weekend, 1,30,000 food packets and 70,000 water containers were distributed.
- UN navy listed its resources in the area as 17 ships, 48 helicopters and 12 fixed wing air craft.
- Thousands of Haitian red cross volunteers and hundreds of red cross red crescent staff from other countries continue their work to help the country heal.

Helicopters transfer injured earthquake victims to hospital ship. Able bodied survivors extricating the living and dead from rubble many buildings collapsed.

**Recovery**

US president Barack Obama announced that former president Bill Clinton and G.W Bush would coordinate efforts to raise funds for Haiti's recovery.

UN development programmes employed hundreds of Haitians to clear roads and to make fuel pellets in cash for work scheme.

**Livestock and biodiversity**

Livestock is mainly constituted by goats about 40-50% and is followed by the pigs, cattle and the chicken.

About 11,000 Haitians fished the nation's 1500km coastline on a full time or part time basis.

**Groups help stray dogs and livestock**

Concept of pets is quite foreign to Haitians.

Robinson and Huerta's groups – worlds two largest for animal welfare, joined a dozen partners to respond to protection and public health issues related to animals in Haiti.

**Very true**

They also have a natural healing power to help people because the love animals have is complete and non judgmental, so you are also helping people when you help the animals.

**Landslides**

**Definition**

- Landslides include mass movements of hills, slopes
- It can be defined as the downward and outward movement of slope forming materials composed of rocks, soils or combination of all these materials along surfaces of separation.
- It can occur by falling, sliding or flowing, either slowly or quickly from one place to another.

**Causes of landslides**

- High rainfall

- Gravitational effect
- Erosion due to deforestation
- Poor construction practices
- Earthquake shaking
- Volcanic eruptions
- Failure of drainage systems
- Landslides are associated with the periods of heavy rainfall or rapid snowmelt and tend to worsen the effect of floods.
- Areas burned by forest or brush fires are particularly susceptible.
- Large amounts of water flowing from driveways, roof areas, roads and other impermeable surfaces can cause slides.

**Effects**

- Property damage
- Injuries
- Water supplies, fisheries, sewage disposal system, forests, dams and roadways can be affected for years after a slide event.
- The negative economic effects of landslides include:
  - Cost to repair structures
  - Loss of property value
  - Disruption of transport routes
  - Medical costs in the event of injury
  - Indirect cost such as lost timeber
- Threat to both economy and humans.
- Huge amount of money have to be spent for damaged properties and infrastructure.
- Relief for people in an affected area incurs huge costs.

Landslides affect fisheries and tourist destinations. Lives are lost, Indirect cost comes from loss of productivity of some crops, damaged infrastructure add decreased property value. Water availability, quantity and quality are affected by landslides.

**Steps for Mitigating Effect of Landslides**

1. **Before landslide**: Be alert, particularly during periods of heavy rainfall or snowmelt or after a wildfire. If you see any signs of landslide or suspect

a landslide may occur, you yourself should make a decision to evacuate. Develop landslide specific planning. Develop evacuation plan. Contact local authorities

2. **During landslide**
   - In prone areas consider leaving in if it is safe to do so.
   - If you are near a stream or channel, be alert for any sudden increase or decrease in water flow and for a change from clear to muddy water.
   - Such changes indicate landslide activity upstream.
3. **After a landslide**
   - Check for trapped or injured persons or animals near the slide without entering the direct slide area.
   - Watch for flooding which occurs after landslide or debris flow.
   - Floods sometimes follow landslide and debris flow because they may both be started by the same event.
   - Check the building foundation, chimney and surrounding land for damage
   - It may help you assess the safety of the area
   - Seek expert advice for evaluating landslide hazard or designing corrective techniques to increase or decrease landslide risk.

**Some facts and fictions about landslides**

**Fiction** : Landslides are caused by earth collapsing in a hole.

**Fact** : Landslides exhibit vertical to horizontal movement down a slope. And most are triggered by heavy rainfall and snowmelt, earthquake shaking, volcanic eruptions and gravity.

**Fiction** : Landslides are caused by human activity.

**Fact** : Landslides are mostly caused by natural forces or events such as heavy rain and snowmelt, earthquake shaking, volcanic eruptions and gravity.

**Avalanches**

Avalanches were first imagined as giant snowballs which increased in size from accretion of underlying snow

What are avalanches?

- They are flows which move under the influence of gravity
- They can be channelized or unconfined
- In this sense, they are similar to pyroclastic flows, debris flows, etc.

- Avalanches have severe consequences
- **Direct effects**
  - impact
  - burial
- **Indirect effects**
  - tsunamis generated if an avalanche enters a lake
  - Avalanche zones

(a) **Starting zone:** where an avalanche is initiated
(b) **Avalanche track:** where it goes
(c) **Runout area:** where it dissipates

(a) Starting zones of avalanches
  - $F_s$ = Safety Factor
  - $F_s$ = (shear strength) / (shear stress)
  - **shear strength:** internal resistance to movement
  - **shear stress:** force causing movement parallel to slope; increases with slope angle
  - If $F_s$ is less than 1, then the slope is unstable and prone to failure

On a slope, gravity has two components, one at right angles to the slope ($g_p$), and the other parallel to the slope ($g_s$). As the slope angle increases, $g_p$ decreases. At a certain point, $g_s$ exceed the shear strength, and failure of the mass occurs.

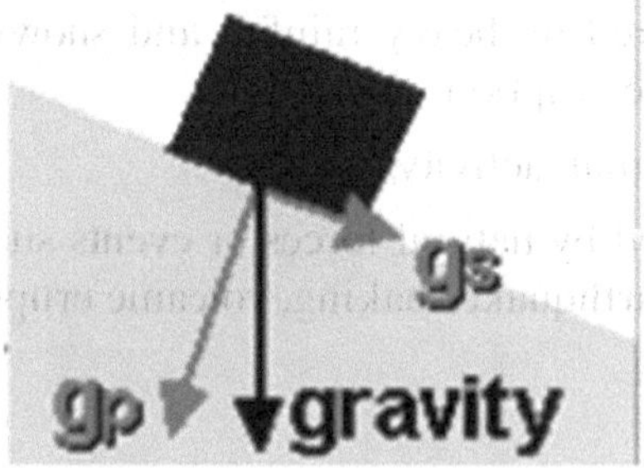


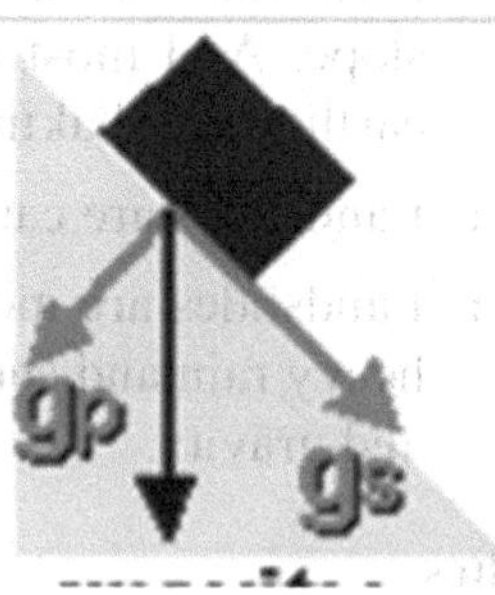


- Layering of snow
- Two weak layers within a slab
- Initial failure - two types

(b) Internal structure of the flow

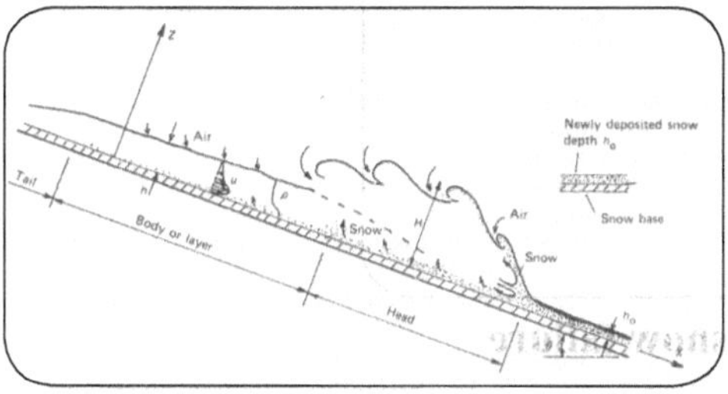

**Snow sheds**

- 2 types of snow avalanche (a spectrum exists)
  - Flow avalanches
  - Airborne powder snow avalanches
- Avalanche flow structure. Note the head, body, and tail of the flow. Vertical and lateral **gradients** in solids (i.e., snow) concentration and in density:
  - A lower dense portion which is highly hazardous and destructive
  - An overlying more dilute portion also can be hazardous and destructive, since it is **turbulent**

**Layering of snow**

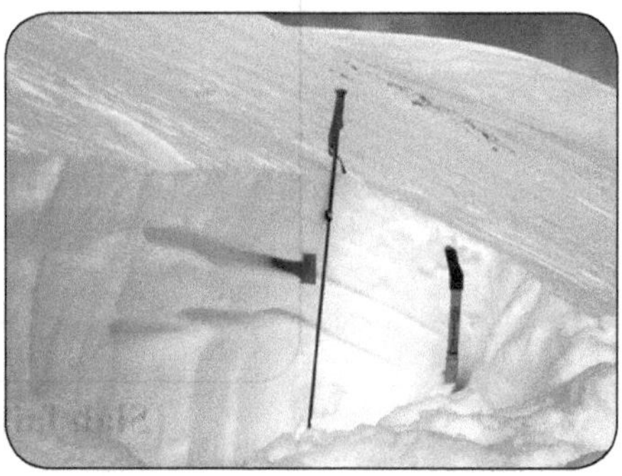

**Two weak layers within a slab**

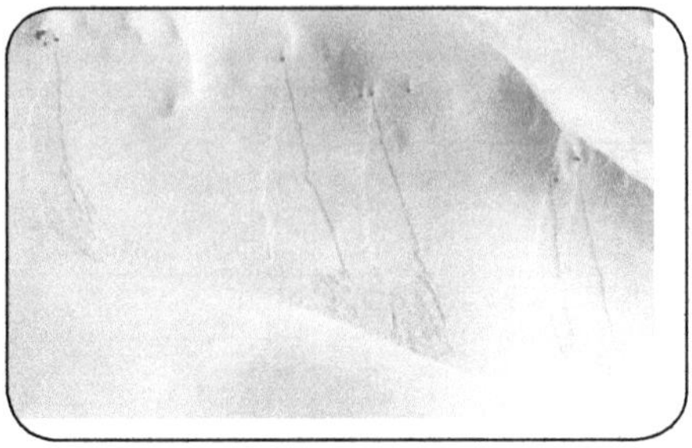

**Loose snow failure**

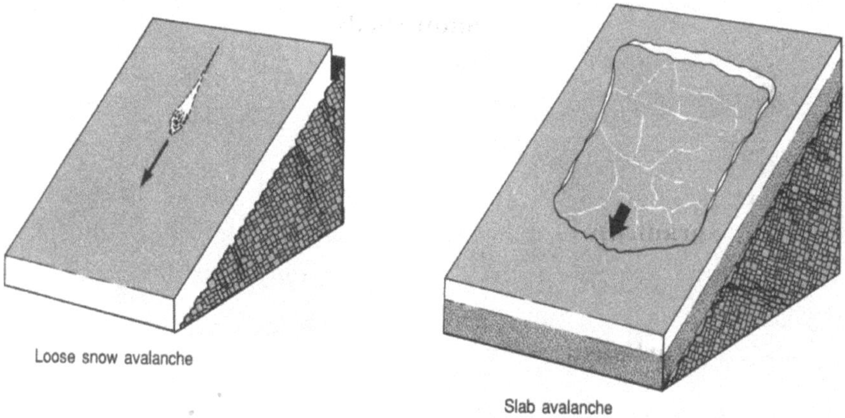


**Initial failure - two types**

**Slab failure**

**Flow avalanches**

- Velocities up to 216 km/hr (60 m/s)
- Flow heights 5-10 meters

- Collisions of particles - granular flow
- Initially tends to slide as a rigid body (similar to a landslide) but rapidly breaks up into smaller particles and becomes a granular flow Interior of the flow

**Airborne powder now avalanches**

- Velocities can exceed 360 km/hr (100 m/s)
- Flow thicknesses may exceed 100 meters

  Essentially a highly dilute density current flowing down an incline:

  - partial entrainment of underlying snow by turbulent, erosive flow
  - dense core small or absent
  - powder avalanches may develop from flow avalanches, but the mechanisms are not well understood

(c) Run out area

- Powder snow avalanches flow around obstacles, while flow avalanches do not
- When powder snow avalanches hit a barrier, the lower dense portion of the flow is **stopped**, while the more dilute cloud behaves like a fluid which can flow around or over the obstacle.

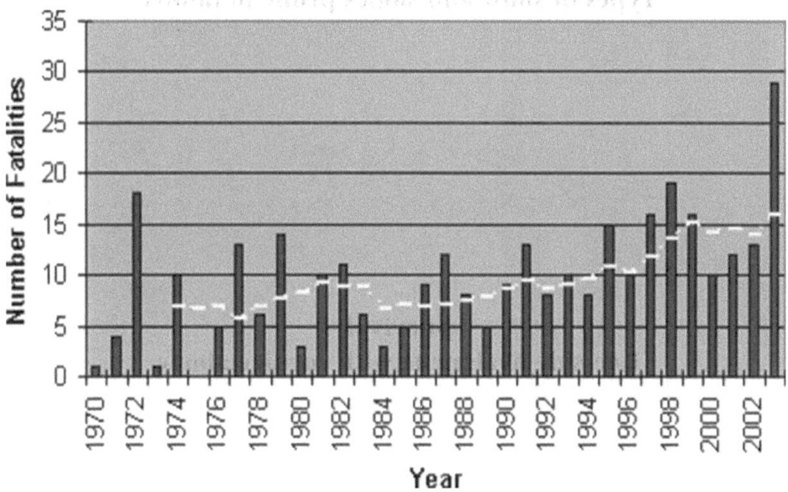

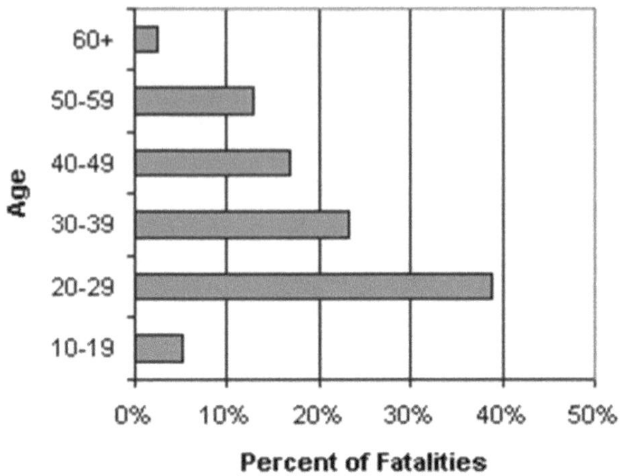


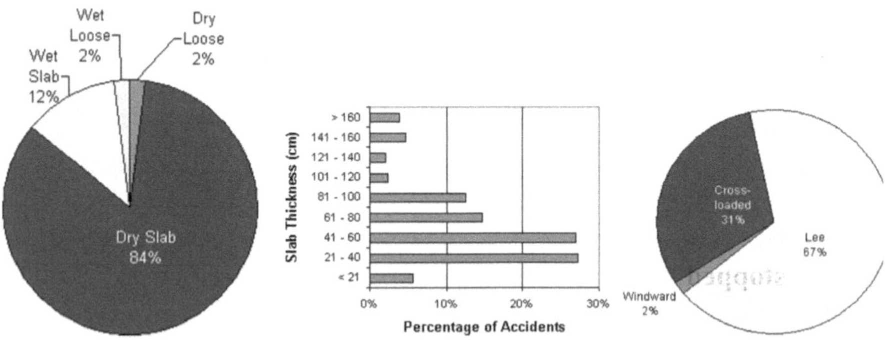


**Types of snow and slopes prone to failure**

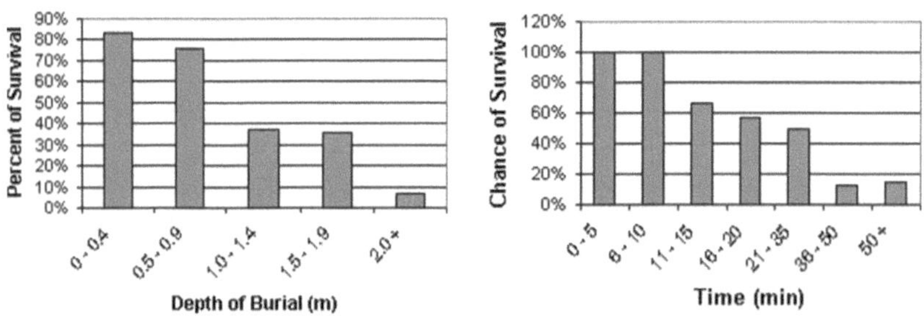


**Survival**

**Lee-side avalanche with cornice above**

### Avalanche causes

- Types of snow and slopes prone to failure
- Survival

### Mitigation

- Avoid steep slopes, gullies
- Close high-hazard areas to reduce risk and vulnerability
- Set off explosive charges to artificially induce avalanches and remove the source material (unstable snow)
- Engineering works

**Reforestation:** To stabilize slopes and snow

**Highways:** Locate to avoid avalanche tracks, use of defense structures: deflectors, mounds, benches with dams. Starting zone defenses. To help reduce avalanches from forming: use of terraces and use of supporting structures.

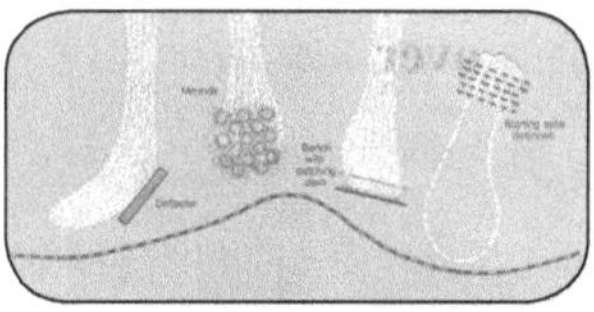

**Use of defense structures**

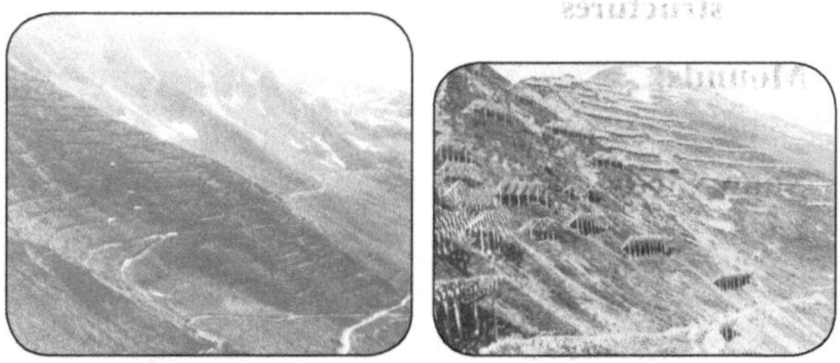

**Terracing in avalanche starting zones (Supporting structures)**

**Some specific examples of mitigation attempts**

**Deflectors:** Must be gradual, otherwise the avalanche will overflow the deflector,

**Arresters:** Arresters are used to slow or stop avalanches. Need adequate height; if too low, flow can accelerate above barrier, increasing damage

**Splitters:** These are placed directly in front of a single object, They redirect and divert the avalanche flow around the structure

**Details of supporting structures** **Arresters** **Splitters**

- **Mounds:** These are used to retard flowing snow at the end of the runout zone
- **Snow sheds:** These sheds allow the avalanche to pass **over** the structure

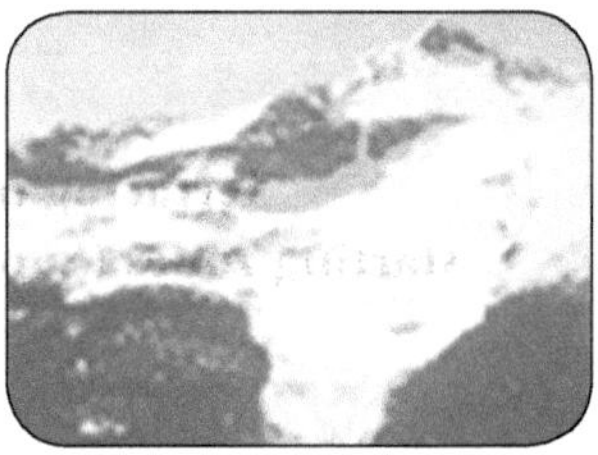

**Use of splitters on ski slopes** **Detail of mounds**

**Volcanic Eruptions**

## Introduction

Opening in planets surface which allows hot magma, ash, gases to escape Word derived from-VULCAN–Roman god of fire, Are creative forces.

**Why do volcanoes?**

Deep with in earth it is so hot that some rocks slowly melt and become thick flowing substance–magma.

Magma pushes through vents & fissures in earth surface

### Types of Volcanoes

- Explosive & non-explosive
- Based on consistency of magma
- Thin magma-non-explosive volcanoes
- Thick magma- explosive volcanoes

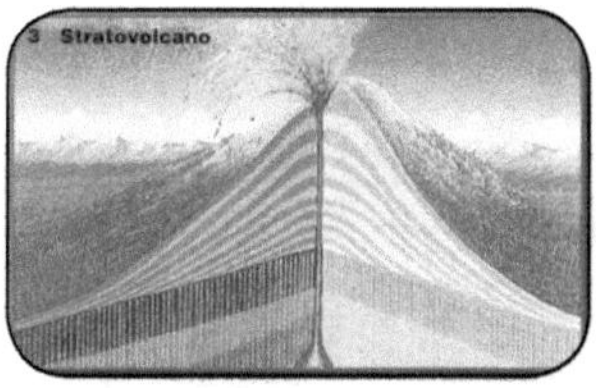

### Kinds

Depends on type of material that erupt

1. Strato volcano – build from eruptions of lava that pile up in layers
2. Cinder cone volcano – build from erupting lava that breaks in to small pieces
3. Shield volcano – formed from eruption of flowing lava that spread out

### Effects of Volcanoes

- Volcanic eruptions alter surface of earth
- Erupt material in to atmosphere – gases ,water vapour that surround the earth
- Winds carry ash to great distance

### Effect on water bodies

- Streams get choked with rock and mud
- Water mixes with rock & mud & create mudflows

### Effect on animals

- Blows down giant trees

- Almost all animals that lives in forest dies
- Death due to lack of vegetation

### Measures

- Volcanic risks should be communicated effectively
- Best warning is one that specifies when & where eruption is most likely to occur
- Most accurate warning are those in which scientists indicate eruption based on significant change in earth's activity, ground deformation & gas emission

## Heat Wave and Cold Waves

### Heat wave

Combination of very high temperature and humidity for a prolonged period.

- Very dangerous situation and major threat to lives
- One of the major disaster
- Sunstroke, severe dehydration, high fever, vomiting, death

### Formation & Effects

Formed when air mass becomes stationary over a region resulting in spell of hot & humid weather. Causes for hot and humid nature of the climate are mainly because of roads, highways, to buckle, Waterlines burst, and Power transformers detonate causing fire.

### Effect on animals

- Damages crops, plants, vegetables
- Lack of adequate drinking water
- Internal body temperature raises,vital organs at rest
- Depletion of salt and electrolytes in the body
- Working under direct sunlight leads to heat exhaustion

### Signs and symptoms

- **Heat exhaustion:** cool, moist, pale/flushed skin, heavy sweating, high fever, vomiting
- **Heat stroke:** hot, red skin, rapid, weak pulse and rapid shallow breathing

**Emergency treatment**

- Quickly cool the body
- Provide cool drinking water
- Electrolytes
- Antiemetics
- Antipyretics

**Measures**

- Keep the animals in shade
- Provide plenty of water to drink
- Avoid strenuous activities
- Keep the animal shelters cool
- Large scale afforestation should receive priority

**Drought Management**

- Avoid mono -cropping
- Choose short duration low water requiring crops
- Drought resistant varieties should be sown
- Sprinkler / drip irrigation
- Weeds should be removed
- Cloud seeding

**Cold Waves**

- Weather phenomenon that is distinguished by cooling of air
- Rapid fall in temperature
- Determined by the rate at which temperature falls and the minimum to which it falls
- Minimum temperature is dependent on geographical region and time of year

**Formation**

Excessive wind chills leading to weather that seems even colder than it is Can be preceded/accompanied by significant winter weather events such as blizzards / ice storms.

### Historical cold waves

| | | |
|---|---|---|
| 2004 | : | North east US |
| 2007 | : | Argentina |
| 2004–05 | : | Southern Europe |
| 2005–06 | : | Eastern Europe and Russia |
| 2007 | : | All of Canada and most of US |
| 2008 | : | Alaska |
| 2009 | : | Europe |

### Effects

- Mandates greater calorie intake
- Lack of adequate drinking water due to freezing
- Hypothermia and frost bite
- Crop failure
- Death due to hypothermia / starvation

### Counter measures

- Suitable stocks of forage must be secured before cold waves
- Livestock must be shipped from affected areas
- Smudge pots can bring smoke that prevent hard freezes
- Vulnerable crops sprayed with water

## Climate Change: Global Warming and its Impact on Animals

### Introduction

Global warming is the term used to describe a gradual increase in the average temperature of the Earth's atmosphere and its oceans, a change that is believed to be permanently changing the Earth's climate forever.

The scientific consensus related to global warming is that the average temperature of the Earth has risen between 0.4 and 0.8°C over the past 100 years.

According to the World Meteorological Organization (WMO), the decade of 1998–2007 is the warmest on record.

**Causes**

The major cause of global warming is the emission of green house gases like carbon dioxide, methane, nitrous oxide etc into the atmosphere.

**Carbon dioxide ($CO_2$):** Concentrations in the atmosphere increased from approximately 280 parts per million (ppm) in pre-industrial times to 382 ppm in 2006 according to the National Oceanic and Atmospheric Administration's (NOAA).

Almost all of the increase is due to human activities .The current rate of increase in $CO_2$ concentrations is about 1.9 ppm/year. Present $CO_2$ concentrations are higher than any time in at least the last 650,000 years.

The major source of carbon dioxide is the power plants. These power plants emit large amounts of carbon dioxide produced from burning of fossil fuels for the purpose of electricity generation.

About twenty percent of carbon dioxide emitted in the atmosphere comes from burning of gasoline in the engines of the vehicles.

**Methane ($CH_4$): It is more abundant in the Earth's atmosphere now than at any time in at least the past 650,000 years (IPCC, 2007). Methane concentrations increased sharply during most of the 20th century and are now 148% above pre-industrial levels.**

- Methane is more than 20 times as effectual as CO2 at entrapping heat in the atmosphere.
- Methane is obtained from resources such as rice paddies, bovine flatulence, bacteria in bogs and fossil fuel manufacture.
- When fields are flooded, anaerobic situation build up and the organic matter in the soil decays, releasing methane to the atmosphere.

**Nitrous oxide ($N_2O$): It has increased approximately 18 percent in the past 200 years and continues to increase . For about 11,500 years before the industrial period, the concentration of $N_2O$ varied only slightly. It increased relatively rapidly toward the end of the 20th century (IPCC, 2007).**

The main sources of nitrous oxide include nylon and nitric acid production, cars with catalytic converters, the use of fertilizers in agriculture and the burning of organic matter.

### Effect of Global Warming on Animals

Animals are essential to maintain the circle of life and the food chain. It is just not the animals alone, insects, reptiles, and the aquatic life are all interdependent on each other, and on the plants and humans as well.

When forests are cleared out to develop more land for domestic constructions, industrial reasons and farming, everything for animals becomes less; food, water, hunting and breeding ground. Loss of habitat also makes these animals vulnerable to being hunted down, when they come close to human habitats searching for food

Loss of habitat is most vividly seen in the Arctic, where global warming is melting the glaciers, pushing the polar bears into extinction.

The melting glaciers have caused water levels to rise in many oceans, threatening to drown many tropical islands and forests that teem with animal life.

Changes in weather patterns and coastlines affect the food patterns of most aquatic creatures.

### Hibernation, Breeding and Migration

It is believed that hibernation and egg laying or animal birth, which is important aspects of animal life, are now happening on an average of 5.1 days earlier per decade.

Early egg laying is one of the reasons why insects like butterflies, and small birds, are disappearing fast in North America, where higher temperatures lead to earlier spring seasons.

### Animals at highest risk

- Polar bears
- Walruses
- Ice seals
- Salmon
- Caribou
- Arctic foxes
- Penguins
- Muskoxen

### Penguins

Rising temperatures are causing the amount of sea ice to diminish, which in turn causes the amount of algae in the water to decrease. Many tiny organisms, including the krill shrimp which forms the foundation of the penguin's diet, and cannot survive without this important food source.

**Trout**

Coldwater fish, such as trout, depend on glacier water to thrive. As temperatures continue to rise, trout stand to lose three-quarters of their current habitat.

**Coral Reefs**

Coral reefs are colorful underwater forests and act as a natural protective barrier for coastal regions.

In one year alone, sixteen percent of the world's coral reefs were wiped out.

**Arctic Foxes**

In recent years, warmer temperatures have driven the arctic fox farther and farther north in search of more suitable, cooler habitat

**Polar Bears**

For polar bears to survive, they need sea ice. Not to eat , but because their primary prey, the ringed seal, requires sea ice as its primary habitat .

Polar bears hunt for ringed seals on this ice and are virtually incapable of successfully hunting seals in open water.

**International Health Impacts**

- Increased epidemics of malaria in Africa
- Increased cerebral-cardiovascular conditions in China
- Increased heat wave deaths in Europe
- Dengue fever in South East Asia
- More flooding and storms

**What can we do?**

The only solution to this problem is to reduce $CO_2$ emissions. This can be done by following measures;

- Walk or use bicycle for smaller distances
- Unplug appliances when not in use
- Turn off lights when leaving a room
- Reuse or recycle as much as you can
- Replace incandescent with fluorescents'
- Install renewable energy systems; wind, solar, geothermal, etc,.

- Transportation can be the part of solution–Reduce frequent vehicle use, Improve vehicle efficiency and De-carbonize fuels.
- A forestation: We should plant more trees so as to counter the increased levels of $CO_2$ and also to restore the normal vegetation.

Environmental Effect on Animals: ***Increasingly***, consumers are concerned that the production of food is undertaken in harmony with the environment. To meet these concerns it is important that farmers produce milk in a way that minimizes any damage to the environment. The biggest potential source of environmental damage is from pollution caused by manures, slurry, silage liquor, etc.

The suggested Good Agricultural Practices for the Environment are set out under the following headings:

- Have an appropriate waste management system.
- Ensure dairy farming practices do not have an adverse impact on the local environment.

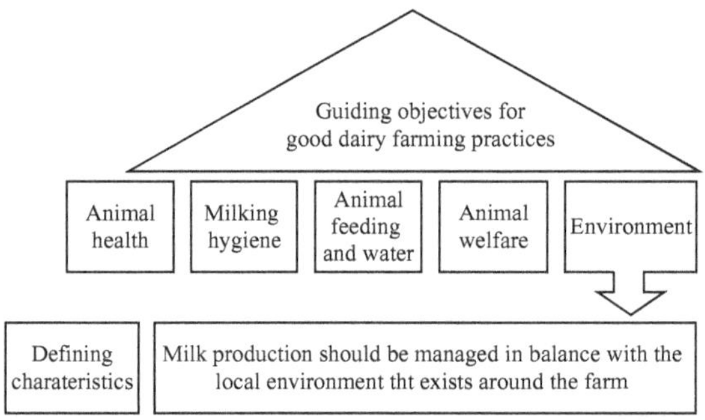


**Have an appropriate waste management system**

**Ensure wastes are stored to minimize the risk of environmental pollution**
Waste storage areas for example: manure heaps and slurry stores, should be sited appropriately. Regularly inspect permanent slurry stores and manure heaps for signs of leaks and impending structural failure to minimize the risk of runoff polluting the environment. Ensure other wastes such as plastic silage wrap are disposed of appropriately to prevent pollution of the environment.

**Manage pastures to avoid effluent runoff by spreading farm manures in accordance with local conditions**: Consider weather conditions and soil types before spreading manures. Use appropriate measures for example. wider buffer zones, to prevent manure from entering watercourses. Consider adopting a manure management plan that identifies areas where there is a high risk of pollution on the farm. If spreading manure to land, follow statutory rates of application. All organic manures–including slurries-should be incorporated into soil as soon as is practical, taking account of soil conditions and prevailing weather conditions. Manure and fertilizer should not be applied to waterlogged, steep or frozen ground where there is a risk of runoff. A simple waste management plan will help identify when, where and at what rate to spread manures, slurry and other organic wastes to minimize the risk of causing pollution. Waste management plans should give due consideration to:

- Avoiding possible pollution of watercourses, ponds, lakes, reservoirs, wells, boreholes, underground water (shallow soils, fissured rock)
- Avoiding potential pollution of habitat areas (e.g. woodlands, protected or recognized flora or fauna zones)
- Ensuring that adequate buffer zones (non-spread areas) are maintained near vulnerable or sensitive areas (e.g water sources, habitat areas)
- Timing and level of application on sloped ground, heavy or impermeable soils and areas subject to flooding
- Optimum application levels on areas that have a high soil fertility status (e.g. high soil phosphorus)
- Current or impending weather and soil conditions at the time of application (frost, frozen ground; heavy rainfall waterlogged soils) national and regional environmental controls

**Ensure Dairy Farming practices do not have an Adverse Impact on the Local Environment**

**Contain dairy runoff on-farm:** Farmers should adopt systems that avoid the potential for the contamination of the local environment. Storage facilities for oil, silage liquor, soiled water and other polluting substances must be located in a safe place and precautions must be taken to ensure that accidents do not result in the pollution of local water supplies. Avoid using or disposing of agricultural or veterinary chemicals where drains, surface water or ground water can enter the local environment.

**Use chemicals (fertilizers, agricultural and veterinary chemicals, pesticides, etc.) appropriately to avoid contamination of the local environment:** The term 'agricultural chemicals' includes farm chemicals (for example pasture sprays, herbicides and grain protectants) as well as detergents and sanitizers used in the dairy. Ensure safe and secure storage of farm chemicals away from the dairy. Use only registered chemicals in the dairy and on the farm; read the label and strictly follow the instructions, including adhering to withholding periods, when using agricultural chemicals. Ensure safe disposal of expired or defective chemicals and empty chemical containers.

**Ensure overall appearance of the dairying operation is appropriate for a facility in which high-quality food is harvested:** To limit the potential adverse impact of dairying on the landscape and to provide a positive image of dairy production, dairy farmers should ensure that access roads to their farms and the farm surroundings are clean, sheds are correctly maintained and that access roads used by cattle are free of effluent.

## Sea Level Rise

### Introduction

- Is a central element in detecting, understanding, attributing and correctly projecting climate change.

### Two types

1. ***Local:*** With respect to a land and due to waves and tides.
2. ***Eustatic:*** World wide and due to changes in ocean basin.

### Causes

- ***Global warming***
- ***Thermal expansion:*** accounts for about half of the SLR.
- ***Land ice melt:*** melting of glaciers is a main contributor.
- ***Subsidence of coastal lands***
- ***Other factors:***
  - Change in land-based water storage,
  - Groundwater extraction,
  - Impoundment in reservoirs,
  - Wetland drainage and deforestation.

### Past, Present and Future

- Average global SLR- 1 to 2mm/year
- India current rise 1mm/year.
- In Bangladesh - 0.3 to 1.5 meters by 2050
- Predicted sea level rise: 0 .03 to 0 .3 m by
- 2040; 0.09 - 0.88m by 2100 by IPCC.
- Extreme low: 0.02m
- Extreme high: 6 m

**Occurs in**

- Maldives and USA
- Greenland and Antarctica
- Low lying islands of Coastal area of Srilanka and islands in Bangladesh.
- Khulna, Karachi, Chennai, Kolkata, Mumbai, Cochin and Lakshadweep.

**Effects of SLR**

- Inundation, salinity intrusions.
- Localized food insecurity.
- Spread water related diseases.
- Vector borne diseases.
- Create drinking/irrigation problem.
- Erode beaches, intensify flooding and increase the salinity of rivers, bays and groundwater tables.

**Animals affected**

- Polar bears
- Sea otters
- Whales and Sharks
- Sea turtles
- Walrus
- Seals
- Penguins
- Sea gulls
- Albatross
- Coral reefs and Fishes etc.,

**Role of Veterinarian**

- Treatment for:
  - Malnutrition
  - Diarrhoea
  - Toxicities
- Control of vectors.
- Shifting of animals to high altitudes.
- Mass feeding of animals.
- Chemoprophylaxis and immunoprophylaxis

### Prevention

- Prevent global warming.
- Reforestation.
- Avoid low lying coastal areas.
- All the countries should work in consensus towards reduction of carbon emission through-
    - (i) Kyoto protocol
    - (ii) Enmod protocol
    - (iii) Montreal protocol

### Adaptation Strategies

- Strengthen disaster warning systems.
- Identify, assess, and evaluate coastal technologies.
- Provide specialized capacity building packages on adaptation.
- Strengthen socio-economic analysis of adaptation.
- Integrated coastal zone management (ICZM).

### Ozone Depletion

**Ozone:** It is a bluish color gas present in the stratosphere. It protects the Earth from the sun's harmful ultraviolet B radiation. Currently, there are two major holes in the ozone layer: one over the North Pole and one over the South Pole.

Each year since the late 1970s, much of the protective elayer of stratospheric ozone above Antarctiva has disappeared during September, creating what is populary called as ozone hole. The Antarctic hole now measures about 9 million square miles, nearly the size of North America. Less dramatic, still significant, depletion of ozone levels has been recorded around the globe. With less ozone in the atmosphere, more ultraviolet radiation strikes Earth, causing more skin cancer, eye damage and possible harm to crops.

The problem: For four months of every year, Antarctica's McMurdo Research Station lies shrouded in darkness. Then the first rays of light peek out over the horizon. Each day, the sun lingers in the sky just a little longer and the harsh polar winter slowly gives way to spring. Spring also brings another type of light to the Antarctic, a light that harms instead of nurtures. In this season of new beginnings, the hole in the ozone layer reforms, allowing lethal ultraviolet radiation to stream through Earth's atmosphere.

The hole lasts for only two months, but its timing could not be worse. Just as sunlight awakens activity in dormant plants and animals, it also delivers a dose of harmful ultraviolet radiation. After eight weeks, the hole leaves. Antarctica, only pass over more populated areas, including New Zealand and Australia. This biologically damaging, high energy radiation can cause skin cancer, injurie eyes, harm the immune system and upset the balance of an entire ecosystem.

### All about the Ozone

**What is ozone?:** How did researchers discover its role in Earth's atmosphere and the devastating consequences of its depletion?

Ozone is a relatively simple molecule, consisting of three oxygen atoms bound together. Yet it has dramatically different effects depending upon its location. Near Earth's surface, where ozone comes into direct contact with life forms, it primarily displays a destructive side. Because it reacts strongly with other molecules, large concentrations of ozone near the ground prove toxic to living things. At higher altitudes, where 90 per cent of our planet's ozone resides, it does a remarkable job of absorbing ultraviolet radiation. In the absence of this gaseous shield in the stratosphere, the harmful radiation has a perfect portal through which to strike Earth.

Although a combination of weather conditions and CFC (Chlorofluoro-carbons) chemistry conspire to create the thinnest ozone levels in the sky above the South pole, CFCs are mainly released at northern latitudes mostly from Europe, Russia, Japan and North America and play a leading role in lowering ozone concentrations around the globe. World wide monitoring has shown that stratospheric ozone has declined for at least decades, with losses of about 10 per cent in the winter and spring and 5 per cent in the summer and autumn, in such diverse locations as Europe, North America and Australia. Researchers now find depletion over the North pole as well, and the problem seems to be getting worse each year. According to United Nations report, the annual dose of harmful ultraviolet radiation striking the northern hemisphere rose by 5 per cent during the past decade.

Ultraviolet radiation is a portion of the electromagnetic spectrum with wavelengths shorter than visible light. The sun produces UV, which is commonly split into three bands – UVA, UVB, and UVC. UVA is not absorbed by ozone. UVB is mostly absorbed by ozone, although some reaches the earth. UVC is completely absorbed by ozone and normal oxygen. UVC is a band of ultraviolet radiation with wavelengths shorter than 280 nanometers.

UVB is a band of ultraviolet radiation with wavelengths from 280–320 nanometers produced by the sun UVB is a kind of ultraviolet light from the sun (and sun lamps) that has several harmful effects particularly effective at damaging DNA. It is a cause of melanoma and other types of skin cancer. It has also been linked to damage to some materials, crops and marine organisms. The ozone layer protects the earth against most UVB coming from the sun. It is always important to protect oneself against UVB, even in the absence of ozone depletion, by wearing hats, sunglasses and sunscreen. However, these precautions will become more important as ozone depletion worsens. UVC is extremely dangerous, but it is completely absorbed by ozone and normal oxygen.

**Destruction of Ozone:** Ozone can be destroyed by a number of free radical catalysts, the most important of which are the hydroxyl radical (OH), the oxide radical (NO) and atomic chlorine (Cl) and Bromine (Br)

### Ozone Depleting Substances (ODS)

Ozone can be destroyed by a number of free radical catalysts, the most important are the

- Chlorofluorocarbons (CFC's): It can stay in the atmosphere for 70 to 100 years, one molecule of Cl destroying up to 100,000 ozone molecules, in 1960's used in refrigerators, air conditioners, spray cans, solvents and foams and phase out by 1996 in developed countries.
- Hydro-chloro-fluro-carbons: First major replacement for CFC, much less destructive by also ozone depleting and reduce HCFC's by 35 per cent by 2004 in developed countries.
- Hydro-fluoro-carbons (HFC): Do not deplete O3, some HFC's have a high GWP
- Halons (Cl-,Br): Contain Br, Cl (in some but not all), F, H (in some but not all), C. Br many times more effective in destroying O3. Used in fire extinguishers and phase out by 1994.
- Hydroxyl radical (OH)
- Nitric oxide radical (NO)
- Methyle Bromide(CH3Br-): An effective pesticide, used to fumigate agricultural soil and products.
- Chlorofluorocarbons (CFC or Freons)
  - Used in refrigerators, air conditioners, spray cans, solvents, foams
  - One molecule of Cl destroying up to 100,000 ozone molecules
  - It can stay in stratosphere for 70 to 250 years
  - Phase out by 1996 in developed countries
- Hydro-chloro-fluorocarbons (HCFCs)
- First major replacement for CFC

- Much less destructive compare to CFC
- Reduce HCFC's by 35% by 2004 in developed countries
- Halons (Br, Cl ,H ,C)
  - Br many times more effective in destroying O3
  - Used in fire extinguishers
  - Phase out by 1994
- Methyl Bromide (CH3Br)
  - An effective pesticide
  - Used to fumigate soil and products
- How Ozone is Being Reduced
- Ozone hole in September 2006
- Effects of Ozone depletion
- Ozone layer absorbs most of the harmful UV-B radiation; more UV-B means:
  - More melanoma and non-melanoma skin cancers
  - Increase eye burning
  - More eye cataracts
  - Suppression of the Immune system
  - Premature aging and brown spots
  - Reduced plant yields
  - Damage to ocean ecosystems
  - Changes in the world's climate
  - Increased global warming(ice melts increase in ocean volume)

**Consequences of Ozone Depletion**

Since the ozone layer absorbs UVB ultraviolet light from the sun, ozone layer depletion is expected to increase surface UVB levels. Possible linked to higher incidence of skin cancer. Lead to decrease of crop yield.

**Effects of ozone depletion:** Increase eye cataracts, suppression of the immune system, increase eye burning, Decrease in crop yields i,e., corn, rice, soybean, damage to aquatic plants essential to ocean food webs, breakdown plastics and other polymers, increased global warming and premature aging and brown spots.

### Controlling Ozone Depletion

Stop producing CFCs, Properly recycle old CFCs, use safe alternatives and educate other governments for environmental policies.

1. Vienna Convention in 1985: framework agreement
2. Montreal Protocol in 1987: Phase-out schedules for CFCs and halons
3. London Amendment in 199: accelerated phase outs; additional CFC's, $CCl_4$
4. Montreal Amendment in 199: finalized phase-out schedules for methyl bromide
5. Montreal Protocol, 1987: Aim: regulate and phase out Ozone Depleting Substances [ODS]

Montreal Protocol Reduce CFC production to 50% of 1986 levels by 1998. The Montreal Protocol on Substances that deplete the ozone layer is an international treaty designed to protect the ozone layer by phasing out the production of a number of substances believed to be responsible for ozone depletion. The treaty entered into force on January 1, 1989.

Current models indicate Ozone recovery by ~ 2050 ± 10

### Role of veterinarian

1. In the ozone depleted area do not allow the animals to expose sunlight when shadow is lesser than the length of body
2. Barriers – clothing, coverings
3. Sun tan lotion
4. Educate the people

**Current situation:** CFCs have been replaced by less damaging hydro-chloro-fluoro-carbons (HCFCs), although concerns remain regarding HCFCs also. In some applications, HFCs have been used to replaced by CFCs, which contain no chlorine or bromine, do not contribute at all to ozone depletion although they are potent green house gases.

# 2

# Man Made Disasters

## Nuclear Disasters

### What is NUCLEAR ENERGY or NUCLEAR POWER?

- It is the energy released in nuclear fission or nuclear fusion.
- Motive power generated by nuclear reactor.
- Where atomic energy of a substance get converted in to electrical energy.

### Nuclear Power Today

- Provides 20% of world's electricity (8% in U.S).
- More than 100 plants in U.S. None built since 1970.
- 200+ plants in the Europe.
- Leader is France, About 80% of its power from nuclear.
- There are 9 nuclear power plants in India, provides 3% of total power generation with a potential total capacity of 4800 megawatts.

### Objectives of disaster management

- Learn to perform rapid assessment of nuclear/radiation events in a disaster situation.
- Describe the different types of radiation particles and waves and their effect on the body.
- Learn specific antidotes and medical interventions for nuclear/radiation terrorism victims.

### Objectives of disaster management

- Learn specific pre-hospital and hospital management strategies including proper notification of radiation disasters.

- Differentiate between radiation exposure and contamination.
- Recognize the characteristic signs and symptoms of acute and chronic radiation syndrome.

**Sources of disaster**

- Operator error in nuclear power reactors.
- Nuclear tests.
- Terrorist attack.
- Excessive radiation exposure.
- Bombs, explosives.
- Radiation therapy-effects mainly by ionizing radiation.

**Effect at 1 km distance** **Effects at 5km distance, Radiation burn. Subcutaneous hemorrhage. Atomic bomb cataract.**

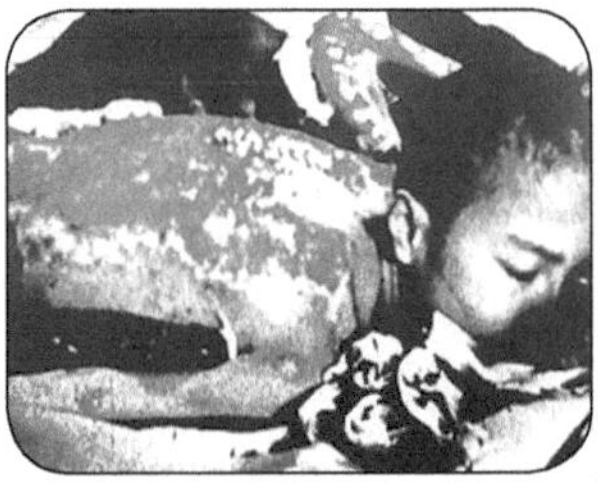

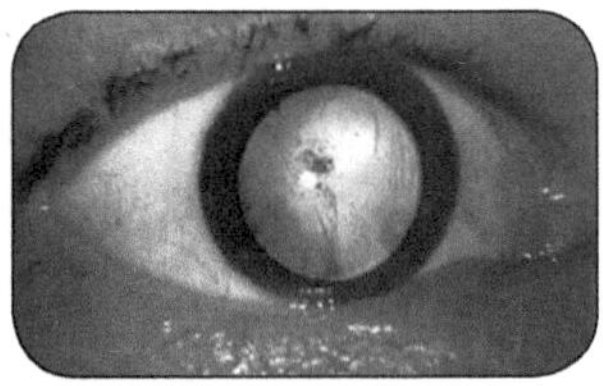

**Hiroshima and Nagasaki incidence, Aug 6,9th.1945**

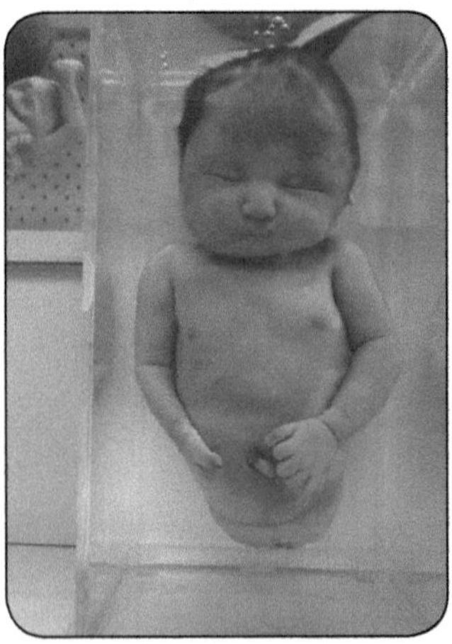

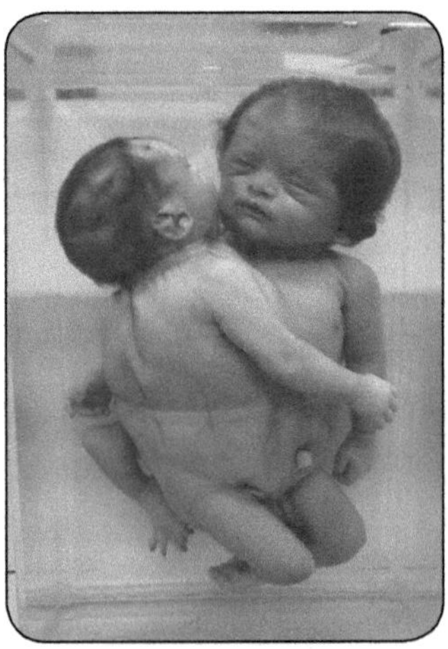

**Malformation of newborns**

## Effects of Hiroshima, Nagasaki

- It is estimated that 5,00,000 or more people died in explosion.
- It destroyed all living and community of living.
- It affected up to genetic level, so that still malformation seeing in newborns.
- Serious injuries like radiation burns, wounds, subcutaneous haemorrhage, radiation cataract finally ended in death.
- High rate of contagious disease conditions.

## Nuclear Power Plant Disaster: Chernobyl, 1986

## Effects of Chernobyl

- Over 2500 public & 15000 animal deaths resulted from the Chernobyl incident.
- The WHO has found a significant increase in cancer in the surrounding area.
- The rate of thyroid cancer is particularly high after the accident because much of the radiation was emitted in the form of iodine-131, which collects in the thyroid gland.

**Nuclear Power Plant Disaster: Chernobyl, 1986**

## Causes for the effects

Radiations emitted by the sources

- Ionizing radiations-
    - Electromagnetic radiation
- X ray, gamma rays.
    - Particulate radiations.
- Alpha, beta, neutrons.

They have high frequency and short wavelength.

## Penetration Abilities of Different Types of Radiation

**Alpha particles:** Alpha particles do not penetrate the dead layer of skin and can be stopped by a thin layer of paper or clothing. If an alpha emitting radioactive material gets inside the body through inhalation, ingestion, or through a wound, the emitted alpha particles can cause ionization those results in damage to tissue.

**Beta particles:** Depending on its energy, beta radiation can travel from inches to many feet in air and is only moderately penetrating in other materials. Some beta radiation can penetrate human skin to the layer where new skin cells are produced. If high enough quantities of beta emitting contaminants are allowed to remain on the skin for a prolonged period of time, they may cause skin injury. Beta emitting contaminants may be harmful if deposited internally. Protective clothing (e.g., universal precautions) typically provides sufficient protection against most external beta radiation.

**Gamma rays and x-rays (photons):** Gamma rays and x-rays are able to travel many feet in air and many inches in human tissue. They readily penetrate most materials. Thick layers of dense materials are needed to shield against gamma radiation. Protective clothing provides little shielding from gamma and x radiation, but will prevent contamination of the skin with the gamma emitting radioactive material.

**Neutrons:** Neutrons also penetrate most materials. They are able to travel many feet in concrete and thousands of feet in air. Thick layers of materials with lots of hydrogen in them (like water or concrete) are needed to shield against neutron radiation. Protective clothing provides no shielding from neutron radiation. Neutrons are not likely to be encountered except in the initial seconds of a nuclear criticality event.

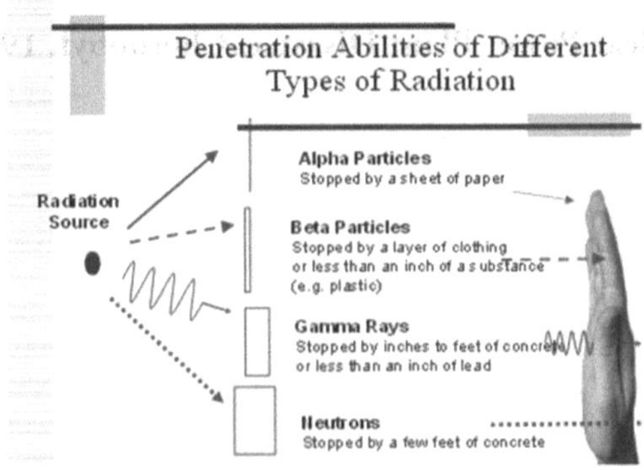

## Factors Determining Radiation Exposure

- Time
- Distance
- Shielding

## Contamination

- Inhaled, ingested, transferred from surface to surface.
- Both internally and externally.
- Radioactive material – can come in any form, including particles similar to dust.

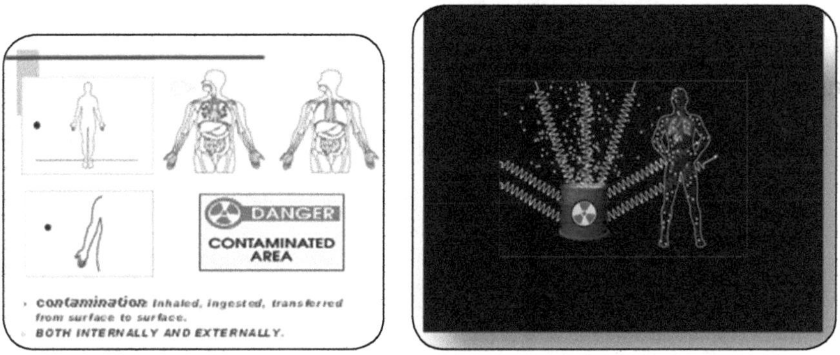


**Picture showing contamination both externally and internally**

## Detecting Radiation

**Radiation cannot be seen, heard, tasted or smelled.**
So, no indication of a leak is noted until symptoms appear. Damage is caused by the energy from radioactive material. The longer the exposure, the worse the outcome will be. But, it can be easily measured. if you have the right equipment.

## Injuries Associated with Radiological Incidents

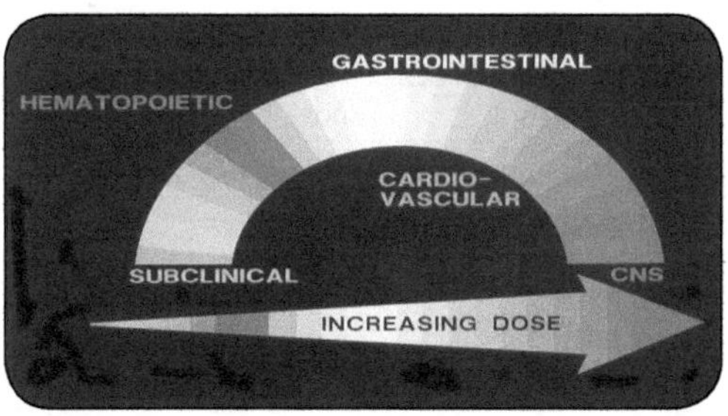


**Acute Radiation Syndrome - A Spectrum of Disease**

- Acute Radiation Syndrome (ARS).
- Localized radiation injuries/cutaneous radiation syndrome.
- Chronic radiation syndrome.
- Combined radiation injuries with
    - Trauma
    - Burns
- Fetal effects.

**Acute Radiation Syndrome**

Stages progress from hematopoietic to gastrointestinal to central nervous system with increasing dose. The absolute lymphocyte count is the best predictor of dose.

**Long-term consequences**

Increase in cancer, especially thyroid cancer. There are chromosomal aberrations, gene mutations, malformations.

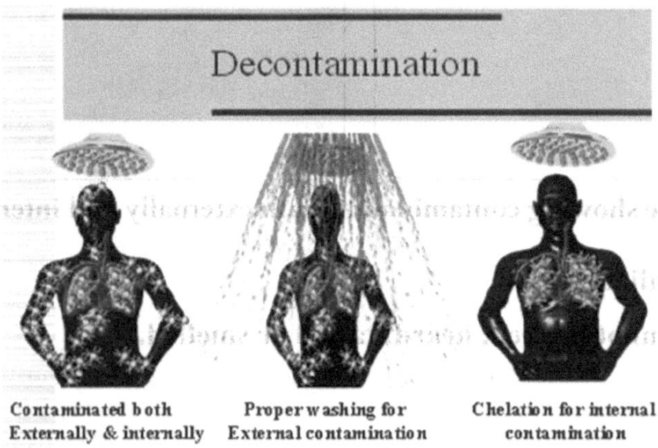


- **Internal contamination** – Radioactive material that has been taken inside the body (often through inhalation).

**Specific Therapy**

| Radionuclide | Therapeutic Approach |
|---|---|
| Tritium | Dilution (force fluids) |
| Iodine-125 or I-131 | KI. |
| Cesium-134 or cesium- 137 | Prussian blue |
| Strontium-89, or 90 | Decrease abs (antacids), blockage (strontium lactate), displacement (oral phosphate), mobilization (ammonium chloride) |
| Plutonium | Zinc or calcium. |

- Diethylenetriamine pentaacetic acid (DTPA)
- These are chelating agents or antidotes for specific radionuclide exposures.
- These antidotes are generally difficult to obtain and each hospital should develop a plan of mobilizing specific antidotes if needed emergently

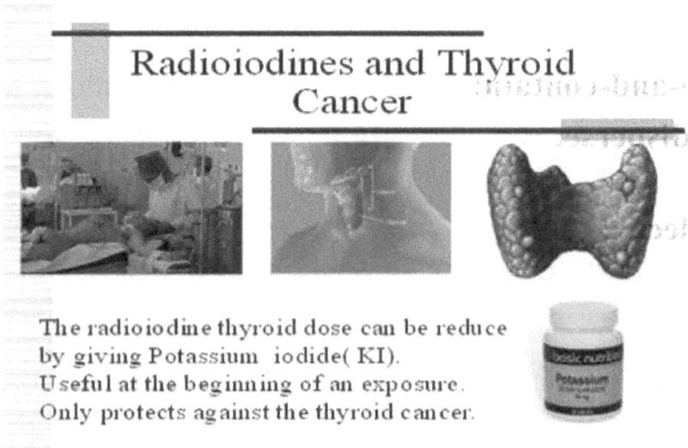


**Nuclear waste management**

Types of radioactive waste (radio-waste)

**Low-level Waste**

- Generated from hospitals, laboratories and industry, as well as the nuclear fuel cycle.
- It has short-lived radioactivity. It is not dangerous to handle.
- Usually it is buried in shallow landfill sites. it is incinerated (in a closed container) before disposal.

**Types of radiowaste**

**Intermediate-level Waste**

- Contains higher amounts of radioactivity and may require special shielding.
- It typically comprises resins, chemical sludge's and reactor components.
- It makes up 7% of all radio waste.
- Generally waste will be disposed of deep underground.

**High-level Waste**

- It contains the highly-radioactive fission products.
- 3% of the volume of all radio waste.

- The separated waste is vitrified by incorporating it into borosilicate (Pyrex) glass which is sealed inside stainless steel canisters for eventual disposal deep underground.

### Nuclear waste management

Principles employed in the management of radioactive wastes:

- **Concentrate-and-contain:** waste is either concentrated or then isolated.
- **Dilute-and-disperse:** is diluted to acceptable levels and then discharged to the environment.
- **Delay-and-decay:** the waste is stored and its radioactivity is allowed to decrease naturally through decay of the radioisotopes in it.

### Anti Nuclear Movement

- Atomic Energy Commission (AEC) established by Congress in 1946 as part of the Atomic Energy Act.
- Manhattan Project for the development of nuclear energy for peaceful civilian purposes at 1953.
- International Atomic Energy Commission 1957.
- Energy Reorganization Act of 1974.
- Nuclear Regulatory Commission.
- Nearly 2/3 of all orders for new plants were cancelled in the late 1970's.

**"if there is an end to this earth that is only by me"-by *ATOM.***

### Chemical Disasters

#### Chemical hazards

1. Chemicals occupy an important segment of our economy and are also source of large benefits to the society.
2. In recent years there has been a rapid increase in the number, variety and complexity of the chemicals being used in the industry and in our daily life.
3. Many of these chemicals are toxic, highly reactive, explosive or inflammable or have a combination of these characteristics and therefore are classified as **hazardous chemicals.**
4. Such chemicals are potential hazards not only to human beings, flora and fauna but to all forms of property and environment as a whole
5. The growth of chemical industries has led to an increase in the risk

of occurrence of incidents associated with hazardous chemicals (HAZCHEM).

**Common causes of chemical accidents**

- Deficiencies in safety management systems.
- Human errors.
- Consequence of natural calamities
- Sabotage activities.
- Chemical accidents result in fire, explosion.
- Toxic release.

**Impact of chemical disaster on life**

- The nature of chemical agents and their concentration during exposure ultimately decides the toxicity and damaging effects on living organisms in the form of symptoms and signs like
- Irreversible pain
- Suffering
- Death.
- Meteorological conditions such as wind speed, wind direction, height of inversion layer, stability class, etc., also play an important role by affecting the dispersion pattern of toxic gas clouds.
- Chemical disasters, though low in frequency, have the potential to cause significant immediate or long-term damage.

**Bhopal gas tragedy**

- In the early morning hours of December 3, 1984 the release of toxic Methylisocyanate gas had occurred suddenly and without warning from the union carbide plant in Bhopal.
- The accident was apparently initiated by introduction of water into Methyl-isocyanate (MIC) storage tank, resulting in an uncontrollable reaction with liberation of heat and escape of MIC in the form of gas.
- This disaster had created thousands of casualties thereby overwhelming local, health and medical resources.
- Safety systems like flare tower (to burn excess of gas), caustic soda scrubber (for neutralization) and the refrigeration unit were either not functioning or inadequate to deal with large volume of escaping chemical.

Of the more than 2 lakh persons exposed to the gas, the initial death toll within a week following the accident was over 2500. In November 1989, Most of the later deaths appeared to be occurring from respiratory complications.

**Sources of chemical disasters**

- Manufacturing and formulation installations including during commissioning and process operations; maintenance and disposal.
- Material handling and storage in manufacturing facilities and isolated storages; warehouses and godowns including tank farms in ports and docks and fuel depots.
- Transportation (road, rail, air, water, and pipelines).

**Causative factors leading to chemical disasters**

- Fire.
- Explosion.
- Toxic release.
- Poisoning.
- Combinations of the above.

**Initiators of chemical accidents**

**Process and safety system failures**

- **Technical errors:** Design defects, fatigue, metal failure, corrosion etc.
- **Human errors:** Neglecting safety instructions, deviating from specified procedures etc.
- **Lack of information:** Absence of emergency warning procedures, nondisclosure of line of treatment etc.
- **Organisational errors:** Poor emergency planning and coordination. Poor communication with public. Noncompliance with mock drills/exercises etc,. Which are required for ensuring a state of quick response and preparedness?
- **Natural calamities:** The Indian subcontinent is highly prone to natural disasters, which can also trigger chemical disasters.

Damage to phosphoric acid sludge containment during the Orissa super cyclone in 1999 and the release of acrylonitrile at Kandla Port, during an earthquake in 2001, are some of the recent examples.

**Terrorist attack/sabotage:** Vulnerability to chemical disasters is further compounded by likely terrorist and warfare activities, which include sabotage and attack on HAZCHEM installations and transportation vehicles.

**Major chemical accidents in India**

| S. No. | Name of the Unit | Date of Accident | Source | Death/Injury/ Missing/Losses |
|---|---|---|---|---|
| 1. | GACL, Vadodara, Gujarat | 05.09.2002 | Chlorine gas-explosion | 4/20/nil |
| 2. | IPCL, Gandhar, Gujarat | 20.12.2002 | Chlorine gas-release | Nil/18 workers & 300 villagers injured. |
| 3. | IOC Refineries, Digboi, Assam | 07.03.2003 | Fire in motor-spirit tank | Nil;Product loss Rs11.55crore |
| 4. | Ranbaxy Laboratories Ltd., Mohali, Punjab | 11.06.2003 | Toluene | 2/19/nil |
| 5. | Anil Enterprises, Zakhira, Rohtak, Haryana | 28.04.2004 | 28.04.2004 | 6/2/nil |
| 6. | Matrix Laboratory Ltd. Unit 1 Kazipally, Medak District, Andhra Pradesh | 05.03.2005 | Sodium hydride | 8/nil/nil |
| 7. | Coromondal Fertilizer Ltd., Ennore, Tamil Nadu | 22.07.2005 | Ammonia | Nil/5/nil |
| 8. | Anjana Explosives Ltd., Peddakaparthi Nalgonda District, Andhra Pradesh | 18.07.2006 | Spillage of hazchem | 5/nil/nil |
| 9. | Reliance Industries Refinery, Jamnagar, Gujarat | 25.10.2006 | Leaked hot vacuum gas oil catches firein air | 2/nil/nil |

**Preventive and regulatory measures of chemical disasters**

- Major Accident Hazard Control System
- Hazard Analysis Studies of Industrial Pockets
- GIS-based Emergency Management System
- Environment Risk Reporting and Information Systems (ERRIS)
- Emergency Response Centres (ERCs) and Poison Control Centres
- National Networking of Emergency Operation Centres (EOCs)
- Control Room Concept.

**Parallel international efforts**

- International Labour Organization (ILO)
- Awareness and Preparedness for Emergencies at the Local Level (APELL) Project

  Suggested elements of an onsite emergency plan

**Plant Emergency Organisation**

- Designated person in charge/alternates.
- Functions of each key individual and group.
- Telephone numbers (office and home) for key people/alternates.

**Plant Risk Evaluation/Information on Preliminary Hazard Analysis**

- Quantity of HAZMATs.
- Location of HAZMATs.
- Special fire-fighting procedures (if any).
- Special handling requirements.
- Type of accidents.
- Safety relevant components.

**Details about the site**

- Location of dangerous substances.
- Seat of key personnel.
- Emergency control room.

**Description of HAZCHEM at the plant site**

- Chemicals (quantities and toxicological data).
- Transformation if any, which could occur.
- Purity of HAZCHEM.

**Likely dangers to the plant**

**Details regarding**

- Warning alarm and safety and security.
- Alarm and hazard control plans in line with disaster control planning, ensuring the necessary technical and organisational precautions.

### Notification Procedures and Communication Systems

- Communication equipment (radios, hot lines, etc.) plant management, local officials.
- Response agencies, neighbouring industries, nearby residents.
- Names and telephone numbers list.
- Central reporting office.

### Emergency Equipment and Facilities

- Fire-fighting equipment.
- Emergency medical supplies.
- Toxic gas detectors (where needed).
- Protective clothing.
- Self-contained breathing apparatus.

### Important roles and responsibilities of various stakeholders

**The chemical industry should fulfill its total obligations as described earlier. The chemical industry shall also specifically address the following:**

(i) Selection of safe technology by industry shall be the prerogative of the industry based on their need, size and availability of inputs as an important preventive measure for CDM.

(ii) On-Site emergency plan and periodic mock drills.

- The district authority is responsible for the Off-Site emergency plan and it shall be equipped with
- Up-to-date MAH units, website, control room etc., with provisions for monitoring the level of preparedness at all times.
- Regular meetings of various stakeholders of CDM will be conducted by administration to review the preparedness for CDM.
- The police will be an important component of all disaster management plans as they will be
- Associated with investigation of accidents/disasters.
- Special training should be imparted to the police personnel for the investigation of a transport emergency involving HAZCHEM.
- The fire services are one of the first responders and shall be adequately trained and equipped.

- In a chemical emergency, the revenue department shall coordinate with other agencies for evacuation, establishment of shelters and provision of food, etc.
- The health department needs to assure that all victims get immediate medical attention.

**List of relevant statues on management of hazardous substances**

- The Environment (Protection) Act, 1986 (amended 1991).
- The Factories Act, 1948 (amended 1987).
- The Inflammable Substances Act, 1952.
- The Petroleum Rules, 2002.
- The National Environment Tribunal Act, 1995.
- The Explosives Act, 1884 (amended till 1983).

**Programmes on cdm**

IDMC 1: 29-30 November 2006
http://nidm.gov.in/idmc/

IDMC 2: 4-6 November 2009,
www.nidm.gov.in/idmc2/

National Workshop on **Chemical Disaster Management**: Preparation of **National Action Plan**, October 2008 (MoEF-NIDM)
**http://nidm.gov.in/cdm**

Training programmes on Chemical (Industrial) Disaster Management: National (2006 onwards) and State level - GIDM, HCMRIPA, YASHADA (2008-09).

**Information management**
Disaster Resource Network
www.idrn.gov.in

Disaster Knowledge Network
www.idkn.nic.in

Indis Data Project: www.desinventar.net, www.emdat.be

## Biological Disaster and Preparadness

BT(Bio terrorism) differs from "conventional" terrorism

- BT attack likely to be covert - first warning is increased demand on medical system from persons with unidentified illness.
- Medical community will be "first responders'.
- Potentially overwhelming impact on health care system.
- Potential for thousands of casualties and civil unrest.
- Need for technical information about biological agent, treatment, prevention and infection control.

## Features of Agents Likely to be Used in a BT Attack

- Easily disseminated and transmitted person-to-person
- Susceptible civilian populations
  - High morbidity & mortality: major public health impact 50kg anthrax spores disseminated over a 2 km line upwind Õ 95,000 deaths and 125,000 total casualties
- Unfamiliar to physicians - difficult to diagnose/treat
- Cause panic and social and economic chaos
- Profound psychological impact on community
- Require special action for public health preparedness

## Agents Most Likely to be used in a BT Attack

- Anthrax (*Bacillus anthracis*)
- Smallpox (Variola major)
- Plague (*Yersinia pestis*)
- Botulism (*Clostridium botulinum*)
- Tularemia (*Franciscella tularensis*)
- Viral encephalitis (Venezuelan equine encephalitis)

## Central Role of Public Health

- Coordinate countrywide preparedness & response
  - Depends on collaboration with key community partners

- Detection and evaluation of biological disaster
  - Requires robust surveillance, epidemiology and disease investigation infrastructure *plus* new detection methods
- Facilitate medical management of exposed persons
  - Treatment, prophylaxis and infection control advice/guidelines
- Provide information to health professionals, government leaders & the public

**Regional Preparedness & Planning Priorities**

- Coordination of regional medical, disaster management and first responder resources and responsibilities
- Inventory and address deficiencies in regional resources
  - Hospital response capacity/preparedness
  - EMS/first responder capacity/preparedness
  - Mass treatment and prophylaxis; mental health capacity
  - Mortuary capacity/preparedness
  - Law enforcement/security
- Protocols to coordinate/engage state & federal resources
- Educate and engage government and community leaders

**Regional Preparedness Planning Activities**

- BT preparedness planning
  - Bioterrorism tabletop exercise with the City.
  - State Terrorism Response Plan
  - Bioterrorism Emergency Response Team: CDC(center for disease control) grant for special surveillance and epidemiology - collaboration with DOH(dept of health)
  - City BT preparedness planning
  - Metropolitan Medical Response System

**Benefits**

- Preparedness for biological terrorism will also prepare our community to respond to inevitable naturally occurring biologic disasters
  - Pandemic influenza

- Large outbreaks of recognized diseases (*E.coli* 0157: H7, meningococcal meningitis, etc.)
- New emerging infections (West Nile Virus, Hantavirus, etc.)
- Other disasters requiring coordination of resources and mass casualties

Picture (Picture shown below as Anthrax) of widened mediastinum representing hemorrhagic mediastinitis which is pathognomonic for inhalational anthrax.

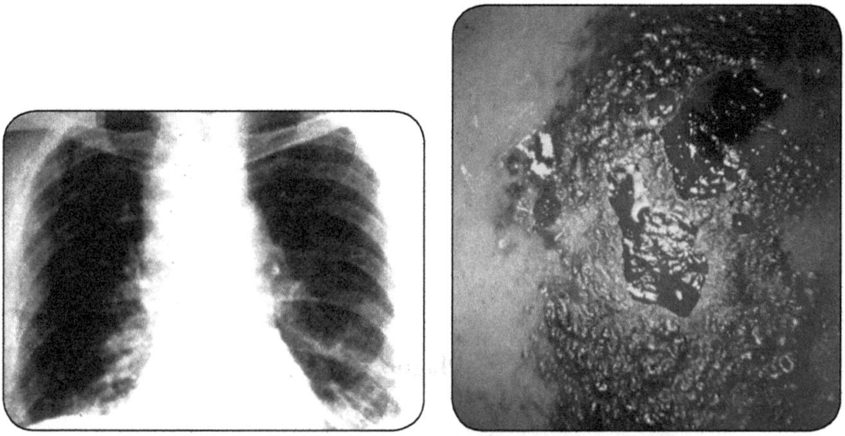

**Anthrax**

- Very rare but most likely form of disease presentation for bioterrorism
- Incubation usually 2-3 days but can be longer
- Flu-like initial symptoms
- Severe symptoms 1-2 days after onset of initial symptoms
- Usually terminal
- Antibiotic treatment before onset of severe symptoms may prevent death
- Incubation period typically 1-6 days
- Fever, malaise, cough leading to severe respiratory distress, shock
- Widened mediastinum on CXR
- Fatality rate 100% untreated
- No person-to-person transmission of inhalational anthrax:
- Early treatment lifesaving: 30-60 day course of ciprofloxacin, doxycyclin, or penicillin
- Post-exposure antibiotic treatment and vaccine.

**Smallpox**

- incubation 7-17 days
  - Acute onset of fever, malaise, headache, backache, vomiting, occasional delirium
  - Transient erythematous rash.

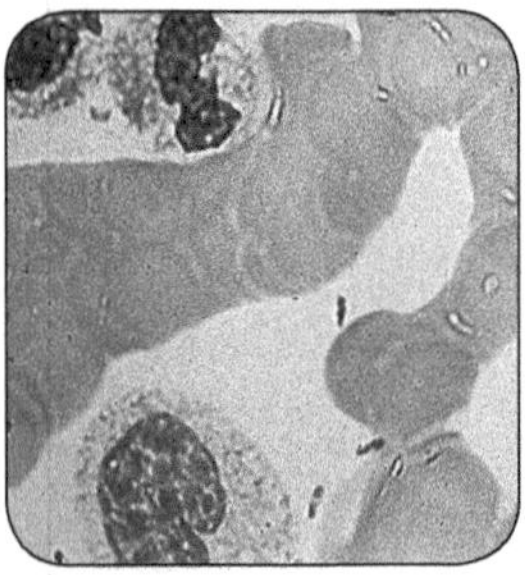

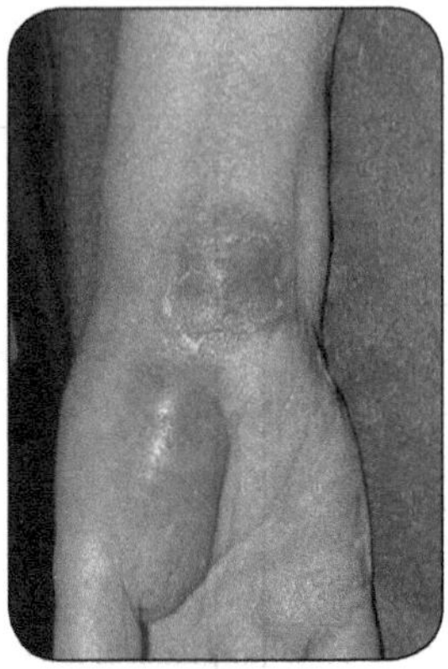

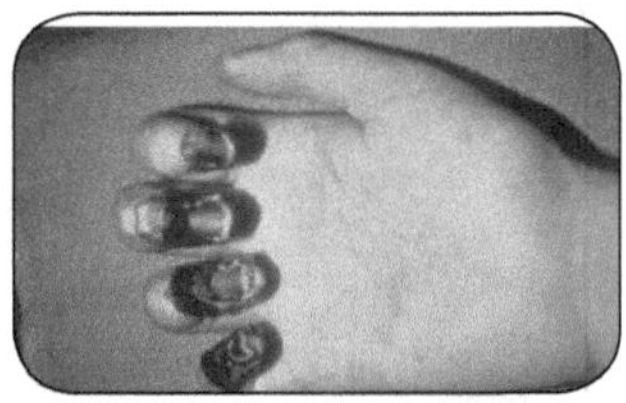

**Plague**

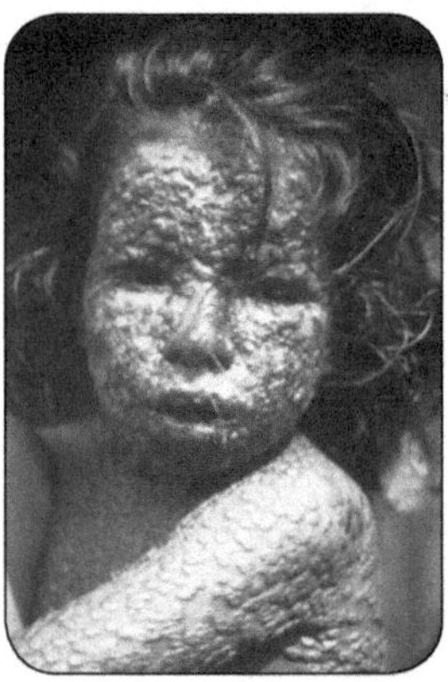

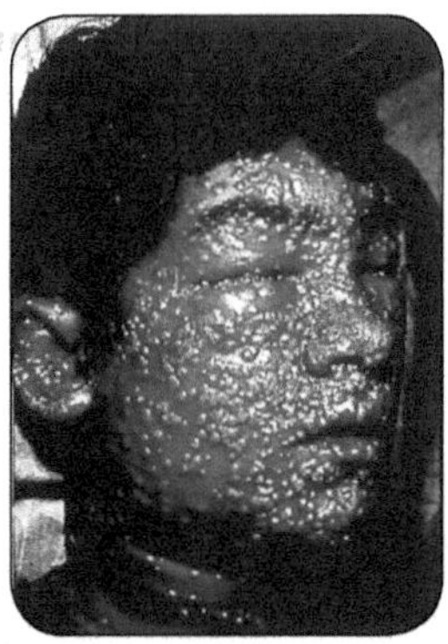

**Smallpox**

**Tularemia**

- Incubation: 3-5 days, range 1-21 days
- Abrupt onset fever, chills, headaches, myalgia, non-productive cough
- Segmental/lobar infiltrates, hilar adenopathy, effusions
- Mortality 30% untreated; < 10% when treated with gentamicin or cipro
- No person-to-person transmission.

**Botulism**

- Inhalation botulism: no natural occurrence, developed as BW weapon
- Toxin from *C. botulinum*: most potent lethal substance known to man (lethal dose 1ng/kg)
- Incubation: 18-36 hours (dose dependent)
- Cranial nerve abnormalities with bilateral descending flaccid paralysis
- Afebrile, alert, oriented, normal sensory exam
- No person-to-person transmission.

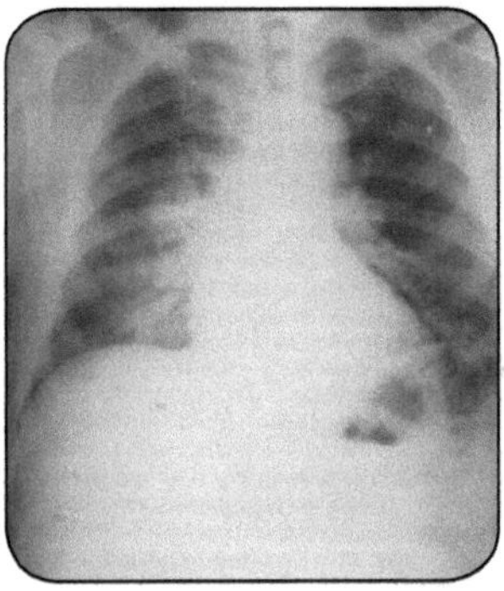

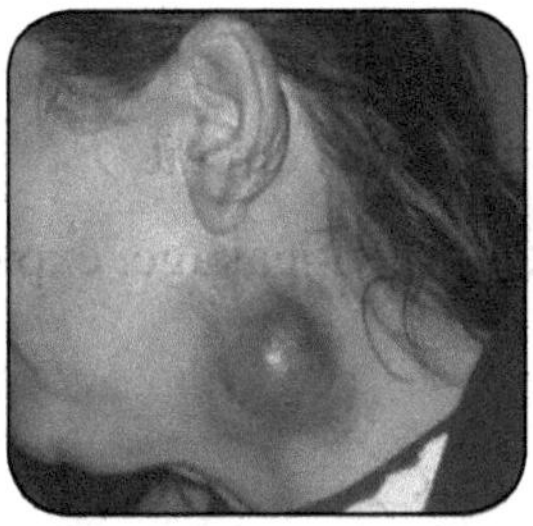

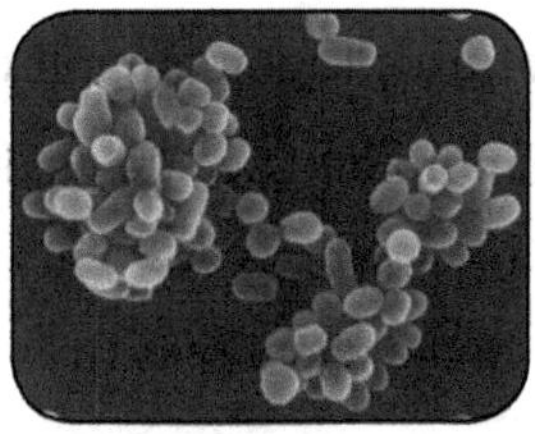

**Tularamia** **Brucella aborts**

**Brucellosis**

- Fever, headache, myalgias, back pain, sweats, chills, malaise
- Osteoarticular infections - large joint or sacroiliac arthritis
- Pulmonary and GI symptoms
- Incubation period 5-50 days
- Diagnosis by culture - requires prolonged incubation
- Standard precautions
- Treatment - six weeks doxycycline + rifampin.

**Glanders**

- *Pseudomonas mallei*
- Fever, headache, rigors, myalgias, pleuritic chest pain, cervical adenopathy, hepatosplenomegaly, generalized papular/pustular rash
- Acute pulmonary disease can lead to bacteremia and sepsis
- Incubation period 10-14 days

- Diagnosis by culture, chest X-ray, serology
- Standard precautions, contact precautions for skin rash
- Treatment - prolonged antibiotic therapy.

**Regional Preparedness Planning and Priorities**

- Protocols to coordinate/engage state & federal resources
- Educate and engage government and community leaders
- EMS (emergency medical system)should be in active state,to cope up,any emergency.

**Building Fire**

Building fire could be a natural or a man made disaster. It's highly unpredictable

**Natural:** Lightening, Electric short circuit.

**Man made:** Accidents due to LPG leakage, explosives.

- Prepration
- In the event of a fire
- Be aware of danger when going into a burning barn:
- Is the electrical supply switched off?
- Is the fire site well ventilated and any potentially toxic fumes dispersed?
- Are remaining roof beams safe?
- Are there any gas bottles?
- The Aftermath
- Three major themes that require immediate attention are identified in case of building fire.

**This comes down to**

**1. People**
**2. Animals and**
**3. The environment**.

**1. People**

- Barn staff has to attend to the animals — both dead and alive.
- For support and guidance, advisory staff has to be arranged, like a veterinarian.

- Electricity people have to be approached for installing new lines and panel boxes to serve the dry barn.

**2. Animals**

**3. Environment**

***General guidelines***

- These could apply to any location, disaster plans like the one required for barn fires are few and far between.
- Disaster plans need to be customized to each farm but there are common elements such as making up the emergency contact list that are common to all emergencies.
- During the process of re-building, buildings must also receive extra attention in terms of fire prevention. New dry walls are added to prevent repetition; retardant materials are to be included in the ceilings and flooring.

**Burns**

- Tissue changes that occur on excessive absorption of heat by skin are known as burns.
- Extent of injury depends on intensity of heat & for which period its applied.

**Types of Burns**

Classified based on depth of tissue changes into 4 degrees of burns.

1. **First degree:** Epidermis. Erythema of skin due to hyperemia of cutaneous vessels.
2. **Second degree:** Coagulative necrosis of epidermal cells with formation of vesicles.
3. **Third degree:** Destruction of dermis & epidermis, accumulation of edematous fluid.
4. **Fourth degree:** Extends to sub cutaneous fascia & deeper tissues like muscles, bones & CNS.

**Effects of Burns**

- If one third to one fourth of body surface is affected even in first or second degree burns death may result within 24 hrs.
- Symptoms seen: Dyspnoea, fall in BP, body temp, traumatic shock.

- In milder cases edema of lungs & nephritis may cause death after several days.

### Treatment

- Dehydration & shock must be treated first.
- Apply emollients.
- Blisters may be ruptured to drain exudates.
- Exposed areas are protected by astringents, antiseptics & anodyne ointments.
- Local analgesics may be incorporated with ointments to control pain.
- Antibiotics to control infections.

### Coal Fire

## Introduction

Coal is a readily combustible black or brownish-black sedimentary rock normally occurring in rock strata in layers or veins called coal beds or coal seams. The harder forms, such as anthracite coal, can be regarded as metamorphic rock because of later exposure to elevated temperature and pressure. Coal is composed primarily of carbon along with variable quantities of other elements, chiefly sulfur, hydrogen, oxygen and nitrogen.

Coal begins as layers of plant matter accumulate at the bottom of a body of water. For the process to continue the plant matter must be protected from biodegradation and oxidization, usually by mud or acidic water. The wide shallow seas of the Carboniferous period provided such conditions. This trapped atmospheric carbon in the ground in immense peat bogs that eventually were covered over and deeply buried by sediments under which they metamorphosed into coal. Over time, the chemical and physical properties of the plant remains (believed to mainly have been fern-like species antedating more modern plant and tree species) were changed by geological action to create a solid material.

Coal, a fossil fuel, is the largest source of energy for the generation of electricity worldwide, as well as one of the largest worldwide anthropogenic sources of carbon dioxide emissions. Gross carbon dioxide emissions from coal usage are slightly more than those from petroleum and about double the amount from natural gas. Coal is extracted from the ground by mining, either underground by shaft mining through the seams or in open pits.

Coal has been mined for over a thousand years as a heating and cooking fuel, but large-scale mining did not begin until the 19th century, in support of the industrial revolution (World Coal Institute, 2000). Although evidence of coal fires from the Pleistocene (Zhang Xiangmin and Kroonenberg, 1996) suggests that such fires are a natural event, strip (opencast) and deep (underground) coal mining by humans has promoted the proliferation and severity of these fires. Such fires burn today in coal seams and culm banks of major coal producing countries including China, the United States, India (Figure 1), and Indonesia.

**Figure 1** Photograph of a shallow coal fire in an Indian coalfield. The coal seam on the left is on fire. Excavated material on the right is being backfilled to seal the goafs (openings) left after mining. Smoke emitting from the fire is high in particulate matter, oxides and dioxides of carbon, nitrogen, and sulfur. In this paper we provide a brief synopsis of the origin of coal mine-related fires, the state of remote sensing technology used in fire detection and prevention, and the thermodynamics of sublimation products from coal fires.

## Origin of Coal Mine Fires

The majority of coal mine-related fires are started by spontaneous combustion, surface fires, and mine-related activities. Spontaneous combustion may be induced by coal fines, oil-soaked rags, hay, manure, and lumber in culm banks (Jones and Scott, 1939; Anthony et al., 1977, p. 29; U.S. Department of Energy, 1993) or by exothermic oxidation reactions catalyzed by oxygen and moisture circulating through coal seam joints. One such reaction is (Limacher, 1963):

$$FeS_2 + (7/2)O_2 + H_2O\ FeSO_4 + H_2SO_4$$

Surface fires ignited by burning trash, lightning, and forest or bush fires may spread to culm banks or coal seams (DeKok, 1986, p. 20; Discover, 1999). The Centralia, Pennsylvania mine fire (Figure 2), one of the worst underground fires in the United States, has been burning since May 1962 (Gessinger, 1990; Memmi, 2000). The fire began as a surface fire when the Centralia Borough Council decided to ignite trash to reduce the volume of and control rodents in an abandoned strip-mining cut used as an unregulated dump at the edge of town. Burning trash ignited the Buck anthracite seam concealed behind the refuse, and the fire spread along the seam to tunnels beneath Centralia (DeKok,

1986, p. 20; Geissinger, 1990; Memmi, 2000). Today, only about 20. people in Centralia remain out of approximately 1100 former residents (Schogol, 2001). Youngstown, Pennsylvania appears to be destined for the “ghost town” fate of Centralia because of the Percy mine fire burning underground there for over 30 years. The Percy mine fire began when burning trash at the surface ignited a coal seam beneath Youngstown (Glover, 1998).

**Figure 2** Northern, eastern middle, western middle, and southern anthracite fields of Pennsylvania. The Centralia underground coal fire (red box), burning since 1962, is in the western middle field (Columbia County

Mine-related activities responsible for starting coal fires include cutting and welding, explosives and electrical work, and smoking which may ignite gases such as methane and hydrogen (Mine Safety and Health Administration, 1996; Pennsylvania Department of Environmental Protection, 2001). Coal fires raging across the Xinjiang autonomous region of northern China, for example, are thought by Chinese officials to have started accidentally in small illegal mineshafts excavated by local farmers (Wingfield-Hayes, 2000). Noxious gases and particulates released by combustion associated with one such fire, the Liu Huangou coalfield fire, are being blown by winds over the region's capital city, Urumqi, one of the 10 worst polluted cities in the world (Wingfield-Hayes, 2000).In China, local miners often use abandoned underground mines for shelter and burn coal to keep warm during the winter. In India, such abandoned mines have been reported to be hideouts for the illegal distillation of alcohol. These kinds of activities are also reported to be responsible for initiating coal mine fires.

## Remote Sensing Technology

Remote sensing technology has made it possible to detect coal fires and study their effects. Thermal and optical images along with field-based measurements (Figure 3) are used to determine the location, size, depth, propagation direction, burning intensity, temperature, and coal consumption of a fire (Zhang et al., 2002, in review; Vekerdy et al., 1999; Prakash and Gupta, 1999). This information has been useful for fighting fires in northern China. Figure 4 shows a processed remote sensing image (Landsat Thematic Mapper (TM) image ) of the Ningxia coal mining area in northwestern China (Prakash et al, 2001). The coal fire areas coded in yellow and red were derived from thermal images. The gray background image is a higher resolution optical image acquired in the near infrared region of the electromagnetic spectrum. The two images have been fused to show the exact locations of the coal fires. The ground control points (pink crosses), measured using the high precision kinematic global positioning system (GPS), were used to transform local coordinates to standard international coordinates. Coal mining and coal dump areas are outlined on this image in green.

**Figure 3** Field-based temperature measurements recorded over fissures associated with underground fires. The fissures form when land subsides due to a reduction in coal volume during subsurface burning.

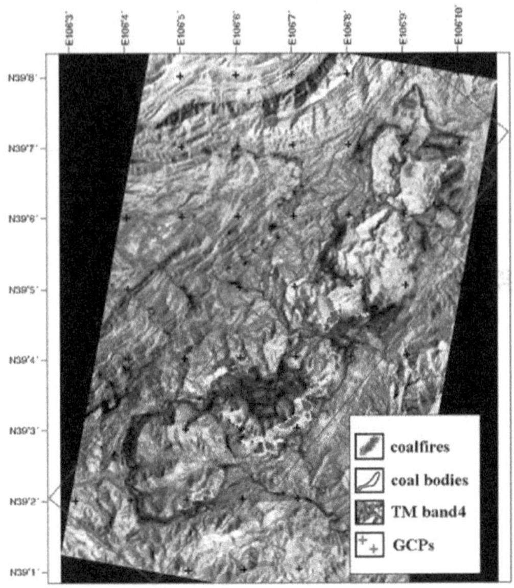


**Figure 4** Processed Landsat TM image of the Ningxia coal mining area in northwestern China. See text for description. (From Prakash et al., 2001).

Subsidence due to underground fires in northwestern China has been identified with thermal, microwave, and optical satellite data (Prakash et al., 2001). Research using synthetic aperture radar (SAR) to identify subsidence is currently being conducted at the International Institute for Aerospace Survey and Earth Sciences (2001; Prakash, 2000).

## Thermodynamics of Sublimation Products

Pollutants associated with coal fires include condensates associated with subsurface combustion. The condensates form when gas exhaled through surficial vents or cracks first cools and then condenses (Lapham, 1980; Stracher 1995). This process is analogous to the exhalation-condensation mechanism by which minerals form in fumarolic or solfatara environments (Stoiber and Rose, 1974). Condensates from anthracite fires in eastern Pennsylvania include (Lapham et al., 1980 and references therein): selenium (Se), sulfur (S) (Figure 5), galena (PbS), orpiment ($As_2S_3$), gypsum ($CaSO_4 \cdot 2H_2O$), mullite ($Al_6Si_2O_{13}$), downeyite ($SeO_2$), salammoniac ($NH_4Cl$), and laphamite ($As_2(Se,S)_3$). Stracher (1995) derived a P-T stability diagram for the condensation of orthorhombic sulfur (Figure 6) from anthracite gas associated with the Centralia, Pennsylvania mine fire using an analytical technique called thermodynamic loop (TL) analysis.

**Figure 5** Anthracite smoker (gas vent) from underground Centralia mine fire. Note sulfur (yellow) condensate around the gas vent. Tip of Glenn Stracher's right shoe (size 7) is in the lower left hand corner of the photo (From Stracher, 1995).

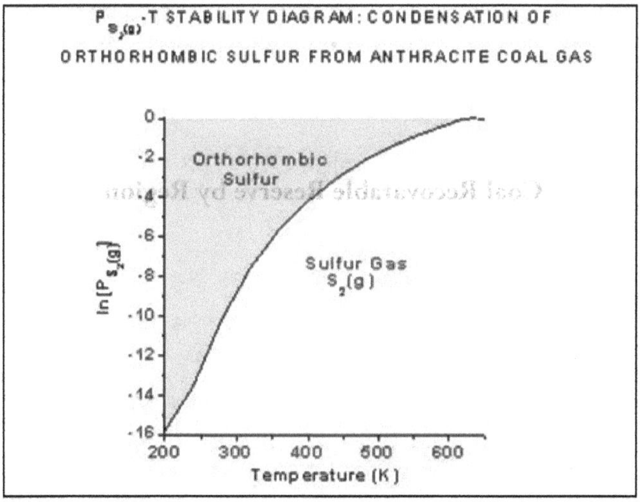


**Figure 6** P-T stability diagram for the condensation of orthorhombic sulfur from anthracite gas associated with the Centralia, PA mine fire (From Stracher, 1995).

This and any such stability diagram serves as an environmental indicator of conditions that tend to favor the condensation of gaseous exhalations as opposed to their absorption into the atmosphere. Stracher and Taylor are currently working on P-T stability diagrams for Selenium (Se) and Galena (PbS).

## World coal reserves

## Coal reserves

World proved coal reserves are currently sufficient to meet 153 years of global production, roughly three times the R/P ratio for oil and gas.

By region, Asia Pacific holds the most proved reserves (46.5% of total), with China accounting for 21.4%. The US remains the largest reserve holder with (22.1%) of the total. North America has the highest regional R/P ratio (356 years).

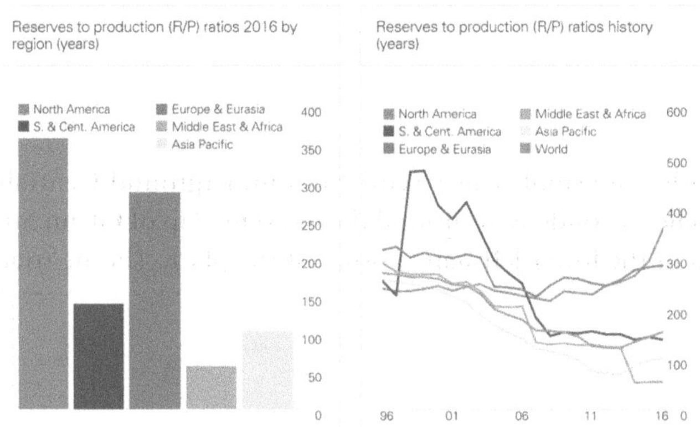


**Coal Recovarable Reserve by Region**

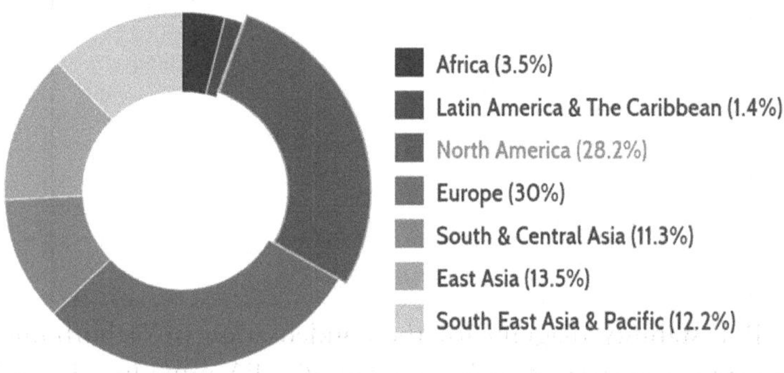


**TOP COAL PRODUCING COUNTRIES**

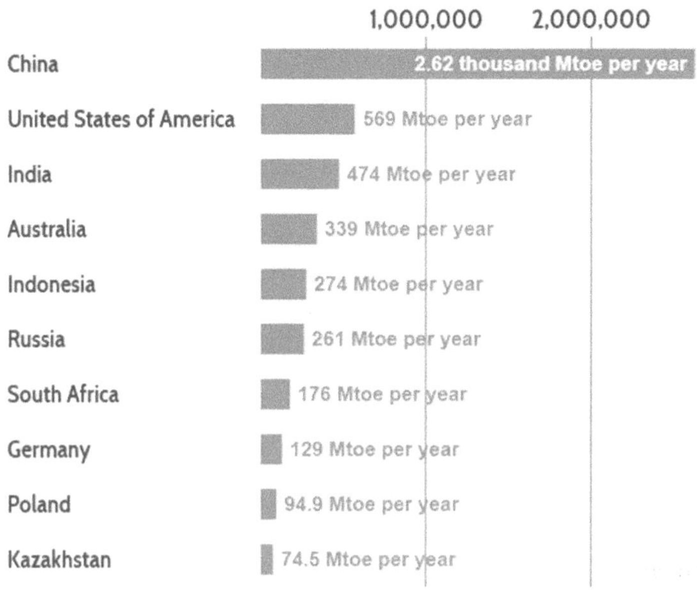


## Methodology

Total proved reserves of coal are generally taken to be those quantities that geological and engineering information indicates with reasonable certainly can be recovered in the future from known deposits under existing economic and operating conditions.

Total proved coal reserves are shown for anthracite and bituminous (including brown coal) and sub-bituminous and lignite.

Reserves-to-production (R/P) ratios represent the length of time that those remaining reserves would last if production were to continue at the previous year's rate. They are calculated by dividing remaining reserves at the end of the year by the production in that year. The R/P ratios are calculated excluding other solid fuels in reserves and production.

R/P ratios are available by country and feature in the table of coal reserves. R/P ratios for the region and the world are depicted in the chart above and the Energy charting tool.

### Coal Reserves in BTUs as of 2009

At the end of 2006 the recoverable coal reserves amounted to around 800 or 900 gigatons. The United States Energy Information Administration gives world reserves as 930 billion short tons (equal to 843 gigatons) as of 2006. At the current extraction rate, this would last 132 years. However, the rate of coal consumption is annually increasing at 2-3% per year and, setting the growth rate to 2.5% yields an exponential depletion time of 56 years (in 2065). At the current global total energy consumption of 15.7 terawatts, there is enough coal to provide the entire planet with all of its energy for 37 years (assuming 0% growth in demand and ignoring transportation's need for liquid fuels).

The 930 billion short tons of recoverable coal reserves estimated by the Energy Information Administration are equal to about 4,116 BBOE (billion barrels of oil equivalent). The amount of coal burned during 2007 was estimated at 7.075 billion short tons, or 133.179 quadrillion BTU's. This is an average of 18.8 million BTU per short ton. In terms of heat content, this is about 57,000,000 barrels (9,100,000 $m^3$) of oil equivalent per day. By comparison in 2007, natural gas provided 51,000,000 barrels (8,100,000 $m^3$) of oil equivalent per day, while oil provided 85.8 million barrels per day.

BP, in its 2007 report, estimated at 2006 end that there were 909,064 million tons of ***proven*** coal reserves worldwide, or 147 years reserves-to-production ratio. This figure only includes reserves classified as "proven"; exploration drilling programs by mining companies, particularly in under-explored areas, are continually providing new reserves. In many cases, companies are aware of coal deposits that have not been sufficiently drilled to qualify as "proven". However, some nations haven't updated their information and assume reserves remain at the same levels even with withdrawals. Collective projections generally predict that global peak coal production may occur sometime around 2025 at 30 percent above current production in the best case scenario, depending on future coal production rates.

## Continental United States Coal Regions

Of the three fossil fuels, coal has the most widely distributed reserves; coal is mined in over 100 countries, and on all continents except Antarctica. The largest reserves are found in the USA, Russia, China, India and Australia. Pakistan also has newly discovered large reserves. Note the table below.

**Proved recoverable coal reserves at end-2006 (million tonnes (teragrams))**

| Country | Bituminous & anthracite | SubBituminous & lignite | Total | Share |
|---|---|---|---|---|
| United States | 111,338 | 135,305 | 246,643 | 27.1 |
| Russia | 49,088 | 107,922 | 157,010 | 17.3 |
| China | 62,200 | 52,300 | 114,500 | 12.6 |
| India | 90,085 | 2,360 | 92,445 | 10.2 |
| Australia | 38,600 | 39,900 | 78,500 | 8.6 |
| South Africa | 48,750 | 0 | 48,750 | 5.4 |
| Ukraine | 16,274 | 17,879 | 34,153 | 3.8 |
| Kazakhstan | 28,151 | 3,128 | 31,279 | 3.4 |
| Poland | 14,000 | 0 | 14,000 | 1.5 |
| Brazil | 0 | 10,113 | 10,113 | 1.1 |
| Germany | 183 | 6,556 | 6,739 | 0.7 |
| Colombia | 6,230 | 381 | 6,611 | 0.7 |
| Canada | 3,471 | 3,107 | 6,578 | 0.7 |
| Czech Republic | 2,094 | 3,458 | 5,552 | 0.6 |
| Indonesia | 740 | 4,228 | 4,968 | 0.5 |
| Turkey | 278 | 3,908 | 4,186 | 0.5 |
| Greece | 0 | 3,900 | 3,900 | 0.4 |
| Hungary | 198 | 3,159 | 3,357 | 0.4 |
| Pakistan | 0 | 3,050 | 3,050 | 0.3 |
| Bulgaria | 4 | 2,183 | 2,187 | 0.2 |
| Serbia | 200 | 1,800 | 2,000 | 0.18 |
| Thailand | 0 | 1,354 | 1,354 | 0.1 |
| Mexico | 860 | 351 | 1,211 | 0.1 |
| North Korea | 300 | 300 | 600 | 0.1 |
| New Zealand | 33 | 538 | 571 | 0.1 |
| Spain | 200 | 330 | 530 | 0.1 |
| Zimbabwe | 502 | 0 | 502 | 0.1 |
| Romania | 22 | 472 | 494 | 0.1 |
| Venezuela | 479 | 0 | 479 | 0.1 |
| All others | 4,691 | 24,111 | 28,802 | 3.1 |
| **Total** | **478,771** | **430,293** | **909,064** | **100** |

## Major coal producers

*See also: List of countries by coal production*

The reserve life is an estimate based only on current production levels and proved reserves level for the countries shown, and makes no assumptions of future production or even current production trends. For comparison, data for the European Union is also shown.

**Production of Coal by Country and year (million tonnes)**

| Country | 2003 | 2004 | 2005 | 2006 | 2007 | 2008 | Share | Reserve Life (years) |
|---|---|---|---|---|---|---|---|---|
| China | 1722.0 | 1992.3 | 2204.7 | 2380.0 | 2526.0 | 2782.0 | 42.5 % | 41 |
| USA | 972.3 | 1008.9 | 1026.5 | 1053.6 | 1040.2 | 1062.8 | 18.0 % | 224 |
| *EU* | 638.0 | 628.4 | 608.0 | 595.5 | 593.4 | 587.7 | 5.2 % | 51 |
| India | 375.4 | 407.7 | 428.4 | 447.3 | 478.4 | 521.7 | 5.8 % | 114 |
| Australia | 351.5 | 366.1 | 378.8 | 385.3 | 399.0 | 401.5 | 6.6 % | 190 |
| Russia | 276.7 | 281.7 | 298.5 | 309.2 | 314.2 | 326.5 | 4.6 % | 481 |
| South Africa | 237.9 | 243.4 | 244.4 | 244.8 | 247.7 | 250.4 | 4.2 % | 121 |
| Indonesia | 114.3 | 132.4 | 146.9 | 195.0 | 217.4 | 229.5 | 4.2 % | 19 |
| Germany | 204.9 | 207.8 | 202.8 | 197.2 | 201.9 | 192.4 | 3.2 % | 35 |
| Poland | 163.8 | 162.4 | 159.5 | 156.1 | 145.9 | 143.9 | 1.8% | 52 |
| **Total World** | **5187.6** | **5585.3** | **5886.7** | **6195.1** | **6421.2** | **6781.2** | **100%** | **142** |

If continuous growth in usage at the rate of the years 2003 to 2006 from the table above (6.0948% pa compound) is assumed, reserves would be exhausted in about 31 years (sum of geometric progression).

## Major coal exporters

**Exports of Coal by Country and year (million short tons)**

| Country | 2003 | 2004 | 2005 | 2006 | 2007 | 2008 | Share |
|---|---|---|---|---|---|---|---|
| Australia | 238.1 | 247.6 | 255.0 | 255.0 | 268.5 | 278.0 | 25.6% |
| Indonesia | 107.8 | 131.4 | 142.0 | 192.2 | 221.9 | 228.2 | 21.0% |
| Russia | 41.0 | 55.7 | 98.6 | 103.4 | 112.2 | 115.4 | 10.6% |
| USA | 43.0 | 48.0 | 51.7 | 51.2 | 60.6 | 83.5 | 7.7% |
| Colombia | 50.4 | 56.4 | 59.2 | 68.3 | 74.5 | 81.5 | 7.5% |
| China | 103.4 | 95.5 | 93.1 | 85.6 | 75.4 | 68.8 | 6.3% |
| South Africa | 78.7 | 74.9 | 78.8 | 75.8 | 72.6 | 68.2 | 6.3% |
| Canada | 27.7 | 28.8 | 31.2 | 31.2 | 33.4 | 36.5 | 3.4% |
| **Total** | **713.9** | **764.0** | **936.0** | **1,000.6** | **1,073.4** | **1,087.3** | **100%** |

## Major coal importers

**Imports of Coal by Country and year (million short tons)[76]**

| Country | 2006 | 2007 | 2008 | Share |
|---|---|---|---|---|
| Japan | 199.7 | 209.0 | 206.0 | 19.4% |
| South Korea | 84.1 | 94.1 | 107.1 | 10.1% |
| India | 52.7 | 29.6 | 70.9 | 6.7% |
| Taiwan | 69.1 | 72.5 | 70.9 | 6.7% |
| Germany | 50.6 | 56.2 | 55.7 | 5.2% |
| **Total** | **991.8** | **1,056.5** | **1,063.2** | **100%** |

## Mitigation

- Do not leave loose coal on the floor and sides of the openings and in the goaves in underground workings and on the coal benches in opencast mines.
- Do not leave the surface cracks due to subsidence without filling. Do not fill the cracks by sand.
- Do not burn dried grasses, etc. on the surface close to the opencast mines, outcrops, subsided areas, abandoned quarries, etc.
- Do not make dumps of carbonaceous shales and pyrite containing rock mass mixed with other rocks.
- Plan for proper and adequate ventilation of the mine workings.
- Plan for minimum possible exposure of coal seams in opencast mines.
- Wherever possible, stop access of air to the active fires as a first step towards mitigation.

## Forest Fire

## Introduction

The most common hazard in forests is forests fire & the most prevalent type of disaster. They pose a threat not only to the forest wealth but also to the entire regime to fauna and flora seriously disturbing the bio-diversity and the ecology and environment of a region.

### Causes of Forest Fire

Forest fires are caused by

- **Natural**
- **Man made**

**Man made causes- when a source of fire like**

- Naked flame
- Cigarette or bidi
- Electric spark
- Any source of ignition comes into contact with inflammable material.

**Classification of Forest Fire**

**Forest fire** can broadly be classified into three categories:

**Natural or controlled forest fire.**

- Forest fires caused by heat generated in the litter and other biomes in summer through carelessness of people **(human neglect)**
- Forest fires purposely caused by **local inhabitants**.

**Types of Forest Fire**

There are two types of forest fire

- **Surface Fire**
- **Crown Fire**

## Surface Fire

- **Crown Fire:** A crown fire in which the crown of trees and shrubs burn, often sustained by a surface fire. A crown fire is particularly very dangerous in a coniferous forest because resinous material given off burning logs burn furiously. On hill slopes, if the fire starts downhill, it spreads to adjacent slope. If the fire starts uphill, there is less likelihood of spreading downwards.

## Crown Fire

- **Vulnerability:** The youngest mountain ranges of Himalayas are the most vulnerable stretches of the world susceptible to forest fires. The forests of Western are more frequently vulnerable to forest fires as compared to those in Eastern Himalayas.

## Preparedness and Mitigation Measures

Forest fires are usually seasonal.

They usually start in the dry season and can be prevented by adequate precautions.

Successive Five Year Plans have provided funds for forests fighting. During the British period, fire was prevented in the summer through removal of forest litter all along the forest boundary. This was called "Forest Fire Line"

This line used to prevent fire breaking into the forest from one compartment to another. The collected litter was burnt in isolation. Generally, the fire spreads only if there is continuous supply of fuel (Dry vegetation) along its path. The best way to control a forest fire is therefore, to prevent it from spreading, which can be done by creating firebreaks in the shape of small clearings of ditches in the forests.

### Precautions

- To keep the source of fire or source of ignition separated from combustible and inflammable material.
- To keep the source of fire under watch and control.
- Not allow combustible or inflammable material to pile up.
- To adopt safe practices in areas near forests viz. factories, coalmines, oil stores, chemical plants and even in household kitchens.
- To incorporate fire reducing and fire fighting techniques and equipment.

### Impacts of Forest Fires on Biological Environment

Forest fires also pose serious health hazards by producing smoke and noxious gases. The burning of vegetation gives **Green house gases** such as carbon monoxide, methane, hydrocarbons, nitric oxide and nitrous oxide, that lead **to global warming & ozone layer depletion**. Consequently, thousands of people suffered from serious respiratory problems due to these toxic gases. Burning forests and grasslands also add to already serious threat of global warming. Recent measurement suggest that biomass burning may be a significant global source of methyl bromide, which is an ozone depleting chemical.

### Forest fire detection

### Mobile Biological Sensors (MBS)

The devices used in this system are **animals** which are native animals living in forests. Sensors (thermo and radiation sensors with GPS features) that measure the temperature and transmit the location of the MBS, access points for wireless communication and a central computer system which classifies of animal actions.

**Methods of Detection**

**1. Animal Behavior Classification (ABC)**

Access points continuously receive data about animal's location using GPS at certain time intervals and the gathered data is then classified and checked to see if there is a sudden movement (panic) of the animal groups.

**2. Thermal Detection (TD)**

The access points get the temperature values from the MBS devices and send the data to a central computer to check for instant changes in the temperatures. Suitable animals for TD method.

**Definition:** Sudden occurrence of unwanted act capable to cause wide spread disruption, deaths or injury. Extensive damage to environment & surroundings Manifests as fire, explosion or toxic release. Requires outside resources to contain it- Oil Sector - inherently hazard prone, large inventory of Petroleum-Highly inflammable

The Exxon Valdez oil tanker scraped along a rocky ocean reef in Alaska cutting open the hull of the ship. Thousands of tons of oil spilled into the ocean - enough to fill a football stadium.

**Oil Sector – inherently hazard prone**

- Large inventory of Petroleum – Highly inflammable
- Processing at high Pressure, Temperature
- Using Hazardous chemicals
- Complexity & Process Integration
- Loss of containment results in Fire/Explosion
- History of Major incidents in India & Abroad.

**Damaging Effects**

- Oil on the water's surface can catch on fire and pollute the air.
- Oil can sink to the ocean floor and destroy the habitats of sea animals.
- Oil can react with oxygen in the air to form acids that are carried by wind and eventually fall back to the ground as acid rain.
- Sea turtles, birds, whales, fish, otters and other animals can become oil-soaked and die.
- Oil washes up on beaches and marshes resulting in life threatening habitats for wildlife species.

- Deer, bears, wolves, dogs, and cats can die from eating oil-soaked beach plants and animal carcasses. Oil clogs the spaces between a bird's feathers, making it impossible for them to fly. Many birds drown and sink in the ocean, never making it to the beaches.

Cleaning oiled birds is not always successful. The birds are weak from struggling in the oil and may be ill from digesting oil while trying to clean their feathers.

**Industrial Disaster is**

- Preventable
- Prevention-The first step
- To contain damages …
- Need to draw a realistic disaster Management Plan

**Disaster Management Plan**

- A consolidated document to cover emergency planning of each plant
- The chain of command & communication enabling emergency procedures for mobilization & evacuation etc.
- Acts as training manual: includes.
- Role of emergency services, know-how & resources.
- Basic Expectations.

**Responsibilities of the occupier**

- Prevent accidents & escalation
- People's protection as the 1st priority
- Emergency actions for the **worst case scenarios**
- Plan, communicate and train
- Feedback for updation & retrain.

**Oil Industry Safety Directorate**

- A Self Regulatory Agency
- A technical directorate under MOP & NG
- Formulates a series of preventive self regulatory safety measures for Oil & Gas industry in India

- Monitors compliance
- Six OISD standards in Petroleum Rules-2002
- Guidelines available on Disaster Preparedness in OISD-145,168 & 206.

**OISD Guidelines on Preventive Measures**

**Areas covered include**

- Exploration & Production (On/Offshore operations)
- Refining, Gas processing & Petrochemicals
- Cross Country Pipelines
- LPG & POL Marketing Installations.

**Safety measures include**

- In-built Safety in Design
- Mechanical integrity
- Operational Safety
- Mechanical Integrity
- Health monitoring of:
- Tanks, Vessels, Pipes, Pumps, Compressors, Heaters, Valves & Fittings
- Onshore/offshore Pipelines
- Firefighting Equip. & System
- Pipelines from corrosion angle
- Integrity of Safety Instrumentation
- Protection to fittings on LPG Trucks.

**How can oil spills be cleaned up?**

- Contain spill with oil booms. Booms are giant Styrofoam logs wrapped in plastic that act like a floating fence.
- Vacuum up spilled oil with skimmer boats. A skimmer is a boat with special equipment that collects oil from the surface of calm waters.
- Absorb the oil with sawdust, straw, foam chips, or other sorbents.
- Use chemicals to disperse the oil into small droplets and let it drift out to sea.
- Biodegrade the oil by spreading microbes on beaches. Microbes are tiny organisms that can digest the oil.

**How can oil tanker spills be prevented?**

Design safer oil tankers.

- Double lined bottom instead of single metal layer.
- Separate compartments for oil storage. In a double-hull tanker, the cargo tanks are separated from the ships outer hull to protect against the impact of an accident.
- Thorough training of tanker crews.
- Develop better emergency procedures.
- Improve navigation skills.

## Air Pollution

### Definition

Air pollution may be defined as the presence of ***one or more contaminants*** or ***combinations thereof*** in the air (outdoor atmosphere), in such quantities and of such durations that tend to be injurious to human, animal or plant life, or property, or which unreasonably interferes with the comfortable life.

### Air Pollutant

It is a substance or effect dwelling temporarily or permanently in the air, which adversely alters the environment by interfering with the health, the comfort, or the food chain, or by interfering with the property values of people.

- A pollutant can be solid (large or sub-molecular), liquid or gas .
- It may originate from a natural or anthropogenic source (or both).

Examples of these are acid rain, ozone in the lower atmosphere, and photochemical smog.

### Health Effects of Nitrogen Oxides

- Short-term exposure at concentrations greater than 3 parts per million (ppm) can measurably decrease lung function.
- Concentrations less than 3 ppm can irritate lungs.
- Concentrations as low as 0.1 ppm cause lung irritation and measurable decreases in lung function in asthmatics.
- Long-term lower level exposures can destroy lung tissue, leading to emphysema.
- Children may also be especially sensitive to the effects of nitrogen oxides.

### Other Effects

- Seriously injure vegetation at certain concentrations. Effects include:
  - Bleaching or killing plant tissue.
  - Causing leaves to fall.
  - Reducing growth rate.
- Deteriorate fabrics and fade dyes.
- Corrode metals (due to nitrate salts formed from nitrogen oxides).
- Reduce visibility.
- Oxides of nitrogen, in the presence of sunlight, can also react with hydrocarbons, forming photochemical oxidants or smog.
- Also, NOx is a precursor to acidic precipitation, which may affect both terrestrial and aquatic ecosystems.

### Sulfur Dioxide

- Ninety-five percent of pollution related sulfur oxide emissions are in the form of sulfur dioxide ($SO_2$), a heavy, colorless gas with an odor like a struck match.
- This gas combines easily with water vapor, forming aerosols of sulfurous acid ($H_2SO_3$), a colorless, mildly corrosive liquid.
- This liquid may then combine with oxygen in the air, forming the even more irritating and corrosive sulfuric acid ($H_2SO_4$).

### Health Effects of Sulfur Oxides

- Sulfur dioxide not only has a bad odor, it can irritate the respiratory system.
- Exposure to high concentrations for short periods of time can constrict the bronchi and increase mucous flow, making breathing difficult.
- Children, the elderly, those with chronic lung disease, and asthmatics are especially susceptible to these effects.

### Health Effects of Ozone

- Ozone acts as a powerful respiratory irritant at the levels frequently found in most of the nation's urban areas during summer months.
- Ozone exposure may lead to:
  - Shortness of breath.
  - Chest pain when inhaling deeply.
  - Wheezing and coughing.

Long-term, repeated exposure to high levels of ozone may lead to large reductions in lung function, inflammation of the lung lining, and increased respiratory discomfort.

## Effects of Air Pollution on Animals

Interest in the effects of air pollution on animals has generally developed as a corollary to the concern about this influence on human health. Studies in which animals have been exposed experimentally to air pollutants have been prompted by the need for specific information concerning the toxicity of various known pollutants. Animal morbidity and mortality following air pollution disasters have been recorded, at least partially, to seek a better understanding of the human injury. There has been a direct concern about the injurious effects of air pollution on animals because of the considerable economic loss which has been claimed in some instances and is potentially associated with this hazard. With the exception of the reports dealing with fluorosis, there is little to be found in the veterinary literature about air pollution as a cause of disease. Most of the information concerning the natural exposure of animals to air pollution is contained in the reports of some major air pollution disasters. E.g: Donora, London, Poza Rica. Recently, considerable information has been reported from medical research laboratories which describe the results of experimental exposure of small animals to various air pollutants.

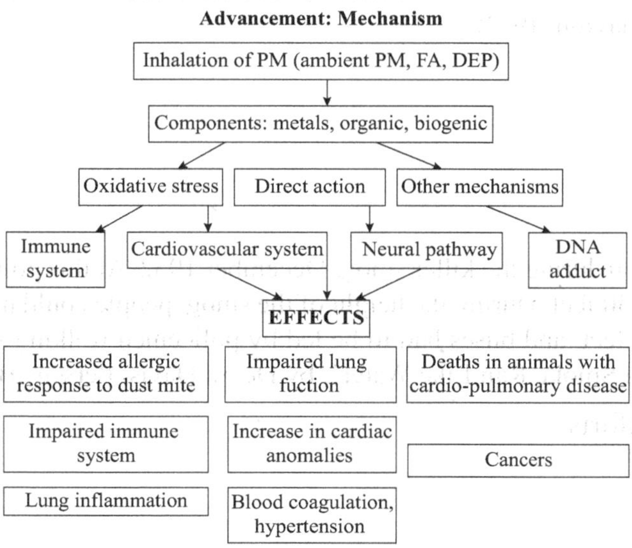

**Major Air Pollution Disasters**

A detailed investigation of both human and animal injury was conducted following the air pollution incident at Donora, Pennsylvania in 1948. A retrospective survey disclosed that an appreciable number of animals were reported to have become ill and that some died during the week of intense smog. The information concerning animal morbidity and mortality was obtained from the owners of both pets and farm animals by personal interviews conducted by registered nurses among the urban population and by a veterinarian among the farmers. Reports obtained by the nurses were subsequently investigated by the veterinarian. Corroborative evidence was sought through conferences with three local veterinarians, technicians in a local dairy-cattle breeding association, two county agents, three local poultry dealers and a slaughterhouse operator. Dogs were reportedly the most susceptible species. Of 229 dogs included in the survey, 15.5 % were reported as having become ill and 10 canine deaths were attributed to the smog. Nearly all of these fatalities occurred among dogs of less than one year of age. The investigators grouped the signs of the canine illnesses attributed to air pollution into three syndromes. Signs of the respiratory syndrome, which occurred most frequently, included cough, sneezing, conjunctival congestion, dyspnoea and nasal discharge. Signs of the digestive syndrome included emesis, retching and diarrhoea. The third syndrome consisted of anorexia which occurred with or without lassitude. A related sulfur compound, hydrogen sulfide, has been held responsible for another major air pollution disaster at Poza Rica, Mexico, 1950 (McCabe & Clayton, 1952). Following this incident, an investigation disclosed that the animal population apparently had been affected. An undetermined number of canaries, chickens, cattle, pigs, geese, ducks and dogs were exposed to the polluted atmosphere at Poza Rica. The reports of animal injury during this disaster disclosed that 100 % of the canaries in the area had died. It was estimated that 50 % of the other exposed animals had died during the period of air pollution.

Central London during the killer smog, December 1952. At this point, visibility is less than 30 feet. During the height of the smog, people could not see their own hands or feet, and buses had to be led by policemen walking with flares. Credit: 'When Smoke Ran Like Water', by Devra Davis, Perseus Books

## Reduction efforts

There are various air pollution control technologies and land use planning strategies available to reduce air pollution. At its most basic level land use planning is likely to involve zoning and transport infrastructure planning. In most developed countries, land use planning is an important part of social policy, ensuring that land is used efficiently for the benefit of the wider economy and population as well as to protect the environment.

Efforts to reduce pollution from mobile sources includes primary regulation,expanding regulation to new sources (such as cruise and transport ships, farm equipment, and small gas-powered equipment such as lawn trimmers), increased fuel efficiency (such as through the use of hybrid vehicles), conversion to cleaner fuels (such as bioethanol, biodiesel, or conversion to electric vehicles).

## Control devices

The following items are commonly used as pollution control devices by industry or transportation devices. They can either destroy contaminants or remove them from an exhaust stream before it is emitted into the atmosphere.

- Mechanical collectors (dust cyclones,multicyclones)
- Electrostatic precipitators
- Baghouses
- Particulate scrubbers
- Low NOx burners
- Exhaust gas recirculation
- Adsorption systems, such as activated carbon
- Cryogenic condensers
- Catalytic oxidizers
- Wet scrubbers
- Dry scrubbers
- Flue gas desulfurization
- Electro-Catalytic Oxidation (ECO)
- Continuous emissions monitoring systems (CEMS)
- Electrostatic-precipitator.

## Most polluted cities

- Air pollution is usually concentrated in densely populated metropolitan areas, especially in developing countries where environmental regulations are relatively lax or nonexistent. However, even populated areas in developed countries attain unhealthy levels of pollution.

| Particulate matter, µg/m³ (2004) | City |
|---|---|
| 169 | Cairo, Egypt |
| 150 | Delhi, India |
| 128 | Kolkata, India (Calcutta) |
| 125 | Tianjin, China |
| 123 | Chongqing, China |
| 109 | Kanpur, India |
| 109 | Lucknow, India |
| 104 | Jakarta, Indonesia |
| 101 | Shenyang, China |

- Carbon dioxide emissions

| Country | Carbon dioxide emissions per year ($10^6$ Tons) (2006) | Percentage of global total |
|---|---|---|
| China | 6,103 | 21.5% |
| United States | 5,752 | 20.2% |
| Russia | 1,564 | 5.5% |
| India | 1,510 | 5.3% |
| Japan | 1293 | 4.6% |
| Germany | 805 | 2.8% |
| United Kingdom | 568 | 2.0% |
| Canada | 544 | 1.9% |
| South Korea | 475 | 1.7% |
| Italy | 474 | 1.7% |

**Environmental impacts of *greenhouse gas* pollutants**

The greenhouse effect is a phenomenon whereby greenhouse gases create a condition in the upper atmosphere causing a trapping of heatand leading to increased surface and lower tropospheric temperatures. Carbon dioxide from combustion of fossil fuels is the major problem.

A number of studies have also investigated the potential for long-term rising levels of atmospheric carbon dioxide to cause increase in the acidity of ocean waters and the possible effects of this on marine ecosystems.

### Water Pollution

## Definition

Its an undesirable change in state of water. It is contamination of water bodies such as lakes, river, oceans, groundwater affecting the organisms, plants & animal in these water bodies &damaging to individual species & population. It occurs when pollutants are discharged directly or indirectly into water bodies without adequate treatment

### Introduction

Major problem in the global context 2nd most important environmental issue next to air pollution Leading worldwide cause of deaths and diseases Accounts for the deaths of more than 14,000 people daily. Estimated 700 million Indians have no access to a proper toilet. 1,000 Indian children die of diarrheal sickness every day 500 million people lack access to safe drinking water. Water is typically referred to as polluted when it is impaired by anthropogenic contaminants and either does not support a human use, like serving as drinking water, and/or undergoes a marked shift in its ability to support its constituent biotic communities, such as fish.

Natural phenomena such as volcanoes, algae blooms, storms, and earthquakes also cause major changes in water quality and the ecological status of water.

**Water pollution cate**Groundwater

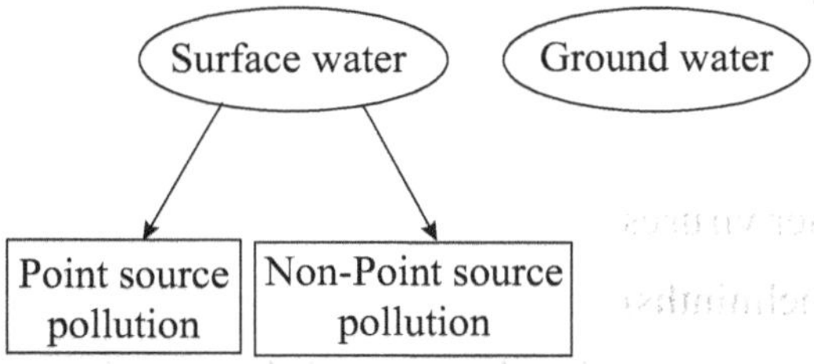


- **Point source pollution:** Refers to contaminants that enter a waterway through a discrete conveyance, such as a pipe or ditch.
- **Nonpoint source pollution:** Refers to diffuse contamination that does not originate from a single discrete source.
- **Groundwater pollution:** Interactions between groundwater and surface water are complex. Sometimes referred to as **groundwater contamination** By its very nature, groundwater aquifers are susceptible to contamination from sources that may not directly affect surface water bodies, and the distinction of point vs. non-point source may be irrelevant.

**Causes of water pollution**

1. Chemicals
2. Pathogens
3. Elevated temperature and discoloration
4. Chemicals and substances that naturally occurring (calcium, sodium, iron, manganese, etc.)

**Oxygen-depleting substances**

Natural (leaves)

Anthropogenic source.

5. **Agricultural:** Commercial livestock and poultry farming, is the source of many organic and inorganic pollutants in surface waters and groundwater
6. **Municipal**: Consists of waste water from homes and commercial establishments.
7. **Industrial**

**Pathogens**

Coliform bacteriaare a commonly-used bacterial indicator of water pollution. Other microorganisms causes health problems include:

*Burkholderia pseudomallei*

*Cryptosporidium parvum*

*Giardia lamblia*

*Salmonella*

*Novovirus* and other viruses

Parasitic worms (helminths)

Pathogen discharges may also be caused by poorly-managed livestock operations.

**Chemical and other contaminants**

**Organic**

(a) Detergents
(b) Disinfection by-products.
(c) Food processing waste.
(d) Insecticides and herbicides.
(e) Petroleum hydrocarbons.

(f) Logging operations
(g) Volatile organic compounds
(h) Chemical found in personal hygiene and cosmetic products.

**Inorganic**

(a) Acids
(b) Ammonia from food processing waste
(c) Chemical waste as industrial by-products
(d) Fertilizers
(e) Heavy metals from motor vehicles
(f) Silt.

**Macroscopic pollution**

(i) Large visible items polluting the water—may be termed "floatables".
(ii) Trash (e.g. paper, plastic, or food waste)
(iii) Nurdles small ubiquitous waterborne plastic pellets
(iv) Shipwrecks large derelict ships.

**Thermal pollution**

1. Thermal pollution is the rise or fall in the temperature of a natural body of water caused by human influence.
2. A common cause of thermal pollution is the use of water as a coolant by power plants and industrial manufacturers.
3. Elevated water temperatures decreases oxygen levels (which can kill fish) and affects ecosystem composition, such as invasion by new thermophilic species.
4. Urban runoff may also elevate temperature in surface waters.
5. Thermal pollution can also be caused by the release of very cold water from the base of reservoirs into warmer rivers.

**Pesticides**

1. Cause of concern as pesticide are mobile in soil
2. Runoff from farms
3. Backyard
4. Golf courses
5. Leechate from landfill site.

**Effects**

- Ecosystem
- Health &reproductive damage in wild life &livestocks.

**Sewage**

1. Inadequately treated municipal sewage is major source of pollution in developing countries.
2. Substantial use of Oxygen for biological degradation there by upsetting the ecological balance of river & lakes.
3. Carries microbial pathogen.

**Nutrients**

**Sources**

1. Domestic wastewater
2. Agriculture run-off
3. Industrial effluent (phosphorus & nitrogen )
4. Fertilizer run-off
5. Manure from livestick.

**Allthese lead to eutrophication**

- **Eutrophication**: Result of nutrient pollution, Release of sewage effluent urban stormwater run-off (carrying excess fertilizers into natural waters). Eutrophication promotes excessive plant growth and decay, favors certain weedy species over others. In aquatic environments chokes aquatic vegetation which disrupts normal functioning of the ecosystem causing lack of oxygen in the water, needed for fish and shellfish to survive.

**Eutrophication of Lake**

**Acidification**

The name given to the ongoing decrease in the pH of the Earth's oceans, caused by their uptake of anthropogenic carbon dioxide from the atmosphere.

**Acidification of surface water, mainly lakes and reservoirs because:-** Transport over long distance of air pollutants such as sulphur dioxide from power plants, steel plants, and motor vehicles.

**Impact of acidification**

The natural absorption of $CO_2$ by the world's oceans helps mitigate the climatic effects of anthropogenic emissions of $CO_2$; it is believed that the resulting decrease in pH will have negative consequences, primarily for oceanic calcifying organisms.

**Quality of life effect**

**Relaxation**

- Recreation
- Aesthetics
- Existence value.

Actual or perceived water pollution is depriving some people use of the water in one or more ways to some extent.

Or, improved water quality would allow more people to use the water more often, in more ways, and/or enjoy it more.

**Economic effect of water pollution**

1. Diminished value of near-water properties
2. Lost business opportunities servicing River users
3. Unavailable for drinking and/or industrial uses; increase treatment costs
4. Physical and mental health care costs and lost productivity resulting from diminished recreation and relaxation.

**Solutions**

1. Education for behavioral change
2. Brochures – many available
3. Events, esp. Earth Day. River clean-ups
4. Presentations to Community Groups (scouts)
5. School programs.

**Education for Behavioral Change**

- It's relatively cheap
- But … it is very difficult and never ending
- Progress is slow.

**Groundwater pollution prevention**

- Monitor aquifers
- Find less hazardous substitutes
- Leak detection systems

- Strictly regulating hazardous waste disposal
- Store hazardous materials above ground.

**Preventing & reducing surface water pollution**

- **Non point sources:** Reduce run –off, Buffer zone vegetation and Reduce soil erosion.
- **Point sources:** Clean water act and Water quality act

## The Impact of Deforestation on Wildlife

### Introduction

The term deforestation refers to the cutting, clearing, and removal of rainforest or related ecosystems into less bio-diverse ecosystems such as pasture, cropland, or plantations.

**The factors responsible for deforestation include**

1. Logging
2. Mining
3. Oil and gas extraction
4. Cattle ranching
5. Agriculture
6. Urbanisation.

**Consequences of deforestation**

1. Environmental Impact
2. Social Impact
3. Environmental Impact.

**Biodiversity**

The process of deforestation in various geographical regions is destroying this unique environment. Consequently, many animals and plants that live in the rainforests face the danger of extinction leading to a diminished gene pool. As the planetary gene pool continues to diminish, there are fewer opportunities for advancements in many fields beneficial to mankind. In particular, medicine may benefit from the cultivation of certain plants that grow only in rainforests.

**Climate change**

- Desiccation of previously moist forest soil
- Dramatic increase in temperature extremes
- Moist humid region changes to desert

- No recycling of water
- Anthropogenic greenhouse effect - less carbon dioxide exchange
- More Desertification
- Soil Erosion.

**Social Impact**

- There was widespread mercury poisoning, pollution from mine sludge and the intensive use of herbicides to control the growth of vegetation near power lines and roads.
- Fish population and agricultural production was declining.
- They changed fish migrating pattern and flooded numerous communities.
- Thus the indigenous people suffered as a result of the actions of the government having made unemployment an even greater problem and aggravated the problem of migrants and homeless people.

## Deforestation and its Impact on Wildlife

### Natural conflicts with Wildlife

As the habitats get dwindled, animals are forced to forage outside their traditional forest range and move into areas populated by humans. It results in fatal encounters with elephants, big cats and snakes in and around degraded forest areas. Species affected by deforestation and habitat destruction include Sumatran tiger, Asiatic lion, Indian Rhino, red panda, Black Buck, Musk Deer, Indian Giant Squirrel and Great Indian Bustard.

### Emerging Infectious Diseases (EIDs)

These are defined as diseases that have recently increased in incidence or geographic range, recently moved into new host populations, recently been discovered or are caused by newly-evolved pathogens. Wildlife EIDs are those which cause morbidity or mortality in wildlife.

Most of the human EIDs are zoonotic: → causing diseases in both animals and humans (e.g. rabies, plague) → caused by pathogens with wildlife reservoir hosts in which they rarely or never cause disease (e.g. Hendra virus disease, Lyme disease) → caused by pathogens that have recently evolved from wildlife ancestors e.g. AIDS.

Intensive livestock production has provided benefits in terms of improved nutrition, but has also created environments favorable to the emergence of diseases.

Forest clearance and climate-induced habitat changes have impacted certain population of mosquitoes, ticks and midges, altering transmission patterns for diseases like malaria and Lyme disease. Kyasanur Forest Disease, vampire bat transmitted rabies, Amphibian Chytridiomycosis.

Two major causes of wildlife disease emergence, as a result of human activity are:

1. Spill-over of pathogens from domestic animals into wildlife populations
2. Anthropogenic movement of pathogens into new geographic locations – a phenomenon termed "pathogen pollution."

## Conclusion

Emerging infectious diseases are considered to be among today's major challenges to science, global health and human development. The growth of human population from approximately one billion in the 20th century to 6.5 billion in the 21st century, has led to major ecological changes and drastic wildlife habitat reduction. As a result of human encroachment on wildlife habitat, there has been emergence or reemergence of zoonotic diseases.

Thus, future collaboration between wildlife ecologists, conservation biologists, environmental biologists, veterinarians and medical scientists, medical microbiologists is required to understand the role of environmental changes in disease emergence. If this important preventive measure continues to be ignored, then human populations will continue to be at risk from pandemic diseases.

## Industrial Wastewater Pollution

Water pollution is the action of environmental contamination with man-made waste into water. The source of this waste could be raw sewage, chemicals, trash, or fertilizer. Water covers over 70% of the Earth surface. Water pollution affects drinking water, rivers, lakes and oceans. This harms human health and the natural environment.

## Types of Water Pollution

### According to number of sources

- Point-source pollution: single source (oil spill).
- Non-point-source pollution: many sources.

### According to the site of affection

- Local pollution: affects immediate area
- Trans-boundary pollution: affects distant area(nuclear waste).

### Causes of Water Pollution

Industry is a huge source of water pollution.

It produces pollutants that are extremely harmful to people and the environment.

### Pollutants from industrial sources include

- **Asbestos:** Asbestosis
  Mesothelioma
  Lung cancer
  Intestinal cancer
  Liver cancer

**Lead:** is harmful to the health of many animals, including humans, as it can inhibit the action of bodily enzymes.

**Mercury:** is harmful to animal health as it can cause illness through mercury poisoning.

**Nitrates:** The increased use of fertilizers causes increased nitrates in the soil and into rivers and lakes, leads to eutrophication which harm marine life.

**Sulphur:** This is a non-metallic substance that is harmful for marine life.

**Oils:** Can stop marine plants receiving enough light for photosynthesis.

It is also harmful for fish and marine birds.

**Petrochemicals:** This is formed from gas or petrol and can be toxic to marine life.

### Minamata: Environmental contamination with methyl mercury

In Minamata, Japan, inorganic mercury was used in the industrial production of acetaldehyde. It was discharged into the nearby bay as waste water and was ingested by organisms in the bottom sediments. Fish and other creatures in the sea were contaminated and residents of this area who consumed the fish suffered from methyl mercury intoxication (Minamata disease). The disease was first detected in 1956 but the mercury emissions continued until 1968.

### Various measures were taken to deal with this disease

- Cessation of the mercury process;
- Industrial effluent control
- Environmental restoration of the bay
- Restrictions on the intake of fish from the bay.

The Minamata disease proved a point towards progress in environment protection measures. This experience clearly showed that health and environment considerations must be integrated into the process of economic and industrial development from an early stage.

## How Can Water Pollution Affect Health?

All types of water pollution are harmful to the health of humans and animals. Water pollution damages our health immediately and after long term exposure.

**Pollutants affect the health of animals as**

Heavy metals from industries accumulate in nearby lakes and rivers.

- Toxic to marine fish and shellfishes, humans eating them.
- Birth defects
- Carcinogenic.
- **Industrial waste:** contains many toxic compounds which damage the health of aquatic animals and those who eat them. Some have a mild effect, other can be fatal.

Cause: Immune suppression<br>Reproductive failure<br>Acute poisoning.

## Treating Industrial Water Pollution

Before raw sewage can be safely released back into the environment, it needs to be treated correctly in a water treatment plant. In a water treatment plant, sewage goes through a number of chambers and chemical processes to reduce the amount and toxicity of the waste.

**The primary phase:** By mechanical filters. Suspended solid particles and inorganic material removed.

**The secondary phase:** By biological filters & processes degrade the organic waste organic matter is removed.

**The tertiary phase:** Almost all solid particles are removed Chemical additives are supplied to get rid of any left-over.

**Industrial wastewater management**

- Command and Control Approach
- Formulate and recommend the effluent standard.
- Monitoring and enforcement.

**Industrial Effluent Standard**

**Enhancement and conservation of National Environmental Quality Act, 1992**

Type of factories and industrial estate designated as pollution sources which require effluent control before discharge to public receiving waters or the environment.

**Sea Accidents**

The Public Information and Education (PIE) sub-committee of the National Disaster Management Council (NDMC) will focus on accidents and emergencies both on land and sea during the month of May.

The Sub-committee in collaboration with key agencies will provide the community with information on how best to prevent and minimize such occurrences and to be equipped in when cases arise.

PIE in collaboration with the Royal Virgin Islands Police Force, BVI Fire and Rescue Services, Virgin Islands Search and Rescue, Virgin Islands Shipping Registry and Conservation and Fisheries' Lifeguard Programme will educate and inform the public about the "do's" and "don'ts" on accident prevention and the systems in place to activate response agencies in a timely and efficient manner.

Police Information Officer Diane Drayton noted the month will be filled with opportunities for the public to become better informed about accident prevention. "We have created a number of informational videos and public service announcements to be aired on both CBN Channel 51 and Jahphix Channel 55 that speak of best practices on the roadways, beaches and on the sea that help to minimize or prevent injuries and casualties," she said.

The videos provide specific instructions both for pedestrians and motorists. Safety tips on pedestrian cross-walks, driving on the roadways with passengers and trucks carrying boxes or materials are also provided. In addition, videos will air safety instructions for swimmers, snorkelers and for those travelling on private vessels.

Interviews are scheduled this month on GIS Radio Report to discuss pedestrian crossings, traffic investigations, boating safety, beach flags, beach safety and the Lifeguard Programme.

During the month, the sub-committee will also be making a special presentation on the 911 Emergency Call-in System and traffic officers will distribute leaflets on traffic tips to drivers.

The Public Information and Education sub-committee, is a part of the National Disaster Management Council and provides information to the public to guard against; reduce the long-term impact and enhance the chances of surviving accidents as well as disasters such as earthquakes, epidemics, fires and hurricanes.

## Injury Prevention and Control in the South-East Asia Region

### Injury Profile in Member Countries

#### Bangladesh

Bangladesh, with a population of 130 million, literacy rate of 55 per cent, and an urbanization of 25 per cent has been witnessing injuries on a very large scale in the last decade. Information on the problem of injuries is totally lacking. However, road traffic injuries are known to be increasing alarmingly with nearly 4 000 fatalities in the year 2000. The number of deaths per 10 000 vehicles is estimated to be 128/10 000 vehicles. The proportional mortality and morbidity from injuries were 8 per cent and 24 per cent respectively, with injuries being reported as the fourth leading cause of deaths. From a hospital-based study, it was shown that one-fifth all admissions were due to injuries. Isolated population-based studies indicate that the death rate from injuries was 40/100 000 population. Among the various national priority problems, road traffic injuries, drowning, violence, burns, occupational injuries, poisoning, and animal-related injuries have been identified as priority injury problems. Bangladesh does not have any specific programmes for injury prevention, except a few isolated and individual efforts by police, transport and other sectors.

#### Bhutan

The health morbidity report for the year 2000 indicates that 3.5 per cent and 3.9 per cent of total health burden is due to injuries as per reports from basic health units. Mortality data for 2000 showed that injuries are the second leading cause of deaths, contributing to 23 per cent of total deaths. Unintentional and intentional injuries accounted for 89 per cent and 11 per cent of total deaths. Among all injury causes, RTIs, fall from height, drowning, landslides and hanging contributed for 42 per cent, 24 per cent, 8 per cent, and 7 per cent, respectively. In recent years injuries have just been recognized as a public health problem and have been included under the Ninth Five-Year Plan. Action has been initiated on emergency medical services training for health workers, establishment of trauma care centres in three regions, traffic safety regulations (vehicle fitness, traffic rules enforcement, license regulations etc.) and advocacy.

#### DPR Korea

The country has been facing a major problem of injuries due to natural disasters from year to year. During October, 2001 alone, nearly 1 000 houses were destroyed and thousands of people lost their earnings and livelihood. The economic loss was estimated to be US$ 48 400 million during the year 2001. The country has been progressing at a rapid pace and injuries have been accorded national priority, as it is considered detrimental to the growth of individuals. Specific days and months have been allocated for injury prevention activities under the united system. First aid hospitals and 24 hours medical cares have taken deep root in management.

**Indonesia**

Road traffic injuries, work place injuries, natural disasters and increasing violence are found to be major injury problems. During 1999, among 40 862 deaths, nearly 30 464 died in road traffic injuries. Agricultural injuries (n=2175), burns (n=1187), falls (n=4400), violence (n=1918) and drowning (n=128) were the other major causes of injury.The national policies and regulations have just begun to identify injuries as a public health problem. The disaster management plan has been fully put into practice to save lives. Several initiatives have been undertaken to reduce transport and workplace injuries. The integrated emergency management system along with training of clinic doctors and development of public centres with centralized ambulance services are some ongoing initiatives.

**India**

As per official reports, nearly 418 505 individuals died in India due to injuries in 1999, an increase of 5.2 per cent compared to the previous year. 62 per cent of these deaths were in the age group of 15–44 years and more among men than women. Injury mortality rates for men and women were 28 and 16 per 100 000, respectively. Transport injuries (100 000), predominantly RTIs (81 036), burns (32 000), suicides (110 000) were the major causes, without inclusion of agricultural and occupational injuries. The injury problem is more acute in rural areas compared with urban areas with significant regional variations.In recent years, the government is making some efforts to handle road and occupational injuries. Injury prevention efforts are made mainly by the police, transport and legal sectors with no involvement of health sector in primary prevention, as the country does not have an injury prevention policy.

**Maldives**

Major data sources in Maldives indicate that with a high motorcycle population nearly 430 accidents occurred in 1999. Drowning is a major problem in the country.

**Myanmar**

Information on injuries is not available for the whole country, except from the Yangon and Mandalay areas. The priority problem in Myanmar has been road traffic injuries and industrial injuries. Injuries contributed to nearly 4 per cent of total deaths and 10 per cent of hospital admissions as per hospital statistics. As per 1993 reports of Yangon General Hospital, among 6 824 injured persons, home injuries, road traffic injuries, violence, occupational injuries, train accidents and water-related injuries accounted for 41 per cent, 27 per cent, 21 per cent, 9 per cent, 2 per cent and 1 per cent respectively. Among the nearly 160 000 vehicles, 70 per cent of are cars with about 27 000 motor cycles. As per the available reports, nearly 1 400 injured persons were registered in YangonCity alone. On an average, factories report 400-500 industrial accidents, with the majority being minor injuries. The health ministry has identified accident prevention as an important area since 1990, though no major developments have been made. Collaborative efforts between the health and related ministries are yet to be identified. A number of legislative and regulatory efforts have been developed and implemented partially in the country.

**Nepal**

The injury problem has been very different in Nepal due to the mountainous and terai regions of the country. As per the annual report of the department of health services, falls, burns and scalds and dog bites were reported in large numbers. Injuries contributed for 2 per cent of the hospital admissions occupying the ninth leading position. Injuries also account for nearly 60-70 per cent emergency room registrations. At the BirHospital, road traffic injuries (80-90 per cent), violence and burns (10-20 per cent) were the principal causes of injury registrations in emergency services. The country has nearly 300 000 vehicles and reported 2 000 accidents with 125 deaths during 2000. With about 4 000-5 000 industries, nearly 2 000 occupational injuries were reported along with 200 fatal injuries. Among the various injuries, falls (1 per cent) and burns (1 per cent) were the major causes. At the same time, nearly 6 000 episodes of violence were also reported in the country with large number of deaths and injuries. Natural disasters are also a major problem in the country.Several initiatives have been made by the country in terms of traffic safety, industrial safety, disaster preparedness and management and injury prevention has been included in the ninth plan.

**Sri Lanka**

As per hospital reports from government health institutions in the year 2 000, nearly 11 per cent of deaths and 16 per cent of admission were due to injuries. If poisoning is included, these figures increase to 17 per cent of deaths and admissions, respectively. Poisoning and burns alone account for 6 per cent and 1per cent of total injury deaths, respectively. Land mine injuries killed a large number of people and injured more than 4 000 people. Burns contributed for nearly 1 per cent of total deaths. A hospital based study revealed that 30 per cent of injuries were due to road traffic injuries. Nearly, 2 150 deaths and 22 000 casualties were due to road traffic injuries during the year 2 000. Among the various categories of people killed and injured in road accidents, pedestrians and two wheeler riders contributed to a major share. Poisoning has been a major problem increasing from year to year with nearly 5 200 completed suicides and 52 700 admissions during 2 000. The commonest cause of poisoning is due to organophosphorus and carbamate insecticides. Sri Lanka has recently initiated multisectoral collaborative activities with the involvement of all partners in prevention. Noncommunicable disease prevention has been the focal point for prevention of accidents and violence in Sri Lanka, with the development of a national committee on prevention of accidents.

**Thailand**

Injuries are a major problem in the country with high death rates due to traffic, falls, occupational injuries, and drowning and intentional injuries. Among the hospital registrations, road traffic injuries contribute to a major share with nearly 13 000 deaths in the year 2 000. Among the various hospital registrations from traffic injuries, injuries to the head and face region are frequent as per trauma registry records. Several risk factors like non-wearing of helmets, drunken driving, risk taking behaviour on roads contribute to large number of road traffic injuries. A survey in the National Hospital of Thailand revealed that road traffic injuries (30 per cent), home accidents (24 per cent), occupational injuries (30 per cent), home accidents (24 per cent), occupational injuries (15 per cent), violence (13 per cent) and others (10 per cent) were the major causes.

The injury situation in Thailand has been analyzed recently with several strengths, weaknesses, opportunities and threats. The Ministry of Public Health has taken a lead role in recent years by strengthening its database, advocating for interventions, evaluating the impact and raising awareness in society. The country has initiated surveillance in selected provinces, developed collaborative programmes and implemented major interventions like introduction of laws to make compulsory wearing of helmet and using seat belt, reduction of drunken driving and others. A national focus has been developed under the Ministry of Health to develop programs.

**Review of injury profiles from Member Countries revealed that:** Injury information is collected by different agencies, mainly by police, legal and labour departments from a legal and criminal point of view.

The available information is grossly under-reported, especially for occupational injuries, burns, drowning and suicides and violence. The reported deaths indicate only the tip of the iceberg with national or regional level data on health sector not being available for any country.

Data needs for prevention require specific focus to identify the epidemiological triad of agent, host and environment and this was not available from the ministry of public health for any type of injury. Country health information systems were not using ICD-10 or E Codes of injury classification, except under the surveillance systems of Thailand.

Several components of vital data like injury causes, hospital rates, rehabilitation needs, burden of injuries and economic impact was not available for Member Countries.

Injury prevention policies and programmes were conspicuously absent in every country and ongoing efforts were crisis-oriented – ad hoc and unscientific in nature.

# 3

# Disaster Management

**Efforts to Mitigate Natural Disaster at National and Global Level**

## What is A 'Disaster'?

- It as 'an event that has occurred unexpectedly with destructive consequences' - (UNOCHA 2005).
- It as 'a calamitous event resulting in loss of life, great human suffering and distress, and large scale material damage' - (IFRC2005).
- None of the international agencies take animals into account in their definitions.

**Disasters can be Divided into Natural and man-made Categories.**

They can also be classified according to scope (international, national or local), rate of onset (sudden or slow) and source.

### Handling Emergencies

Is the discipline of dealing with and avoiding risks, or is a discipline that involves preparing for disaster before it occurs.

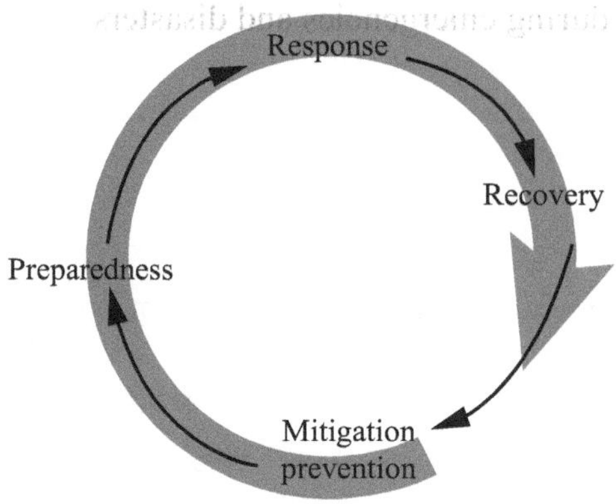


**Cycle of disaster management**

**Mitigation :** The impact of disasters can be reduced before strike, by building certain defenses and implementing appropriate policies.

**Preparedness :** Communication plans with easily understandable terminology and methods. Proper maintenance and training of emergency services, including mass human resources such as community emergency response teams. Development and exercise of emergency population warning methods combined with emergency shelters and evacuation plans.

**Response :** The response phase includes the mobilization of the necessary emergency services and first responders in the disaster area. This is likely to include a first wave of core emergency services, such as firefighters, police and ambulance crews. When conducted as a military operation, it is termed Disaster Relief Operation (DRO).

**Recovery:** The aim of the recovery phase is to restore the affected area to its previous state. It differs from the response phase in its focus; recovery efforts are concerned with issues and decisions that must be made after immediate needs are addressed.

### Risk Identification

- Monitoring
- Early warnings for weather water or climate related disasters
- Adaptation measures
- Vulnerability assessment and Hazard analysis

## International Organizations

### International Association of Emergency Managers

The International Association of Emergency Managers (IAEM) is a non-profit educational organization dedicated to promoting the goals of saving lives and protecting property during emergencies and disasters.
The mission of IAEM is to serve its members by providing information, networking and professional opportunities, and to advance the emergency management profession.

### Red Cross/Red Crescent

- National Red Cross/Red Crescent societies often have pivotal roles in responding to emergencies.
- Additionally, the International Federation of Red Cross and Red Crescent Societies (IFRC or "The Federation") may deploy assessment teams to the affected country. They specialize in the recovery component of the emergency management framework.

**Operational meteorological satellites, both polar-orbiting and geostationary**

- GOES10, GOES-1, NOAA-15, NOAA-16 and NOAA-17 operated by the United States;
- GMS5 operated by Japan;
- GOMS N1, METEOR 2-20, METEOR 2-21, METEOR 3-5 and METEOR 3M N1 operated by the Russian Federation;
- Meteosat5, Meteosat-6 and Meteosat-7 operated by EUMETSAT;
- FY-2B, FY-1C, FY-1D operated by China.

**Additional Satellites in Orbit or in Commissioning**

- GOES-8, GOES-9, and GOES-11 operated by the United States,
- MSG-1 operated by EUMETSAT, R&D satellites,
- NASA's Aqua, Terra, NPP, TRMM, QuikSCAT and GPM missions,
- ESA's ENVISAT, ERS-1 and ERS-2 missions,
- NASDA's ADEOS II and GCOM series,
- Rosaviakosmos's research instruments on board ROSHYDROMET's operational METEOR 3M N1 satellite, as well as on its future Ocean series and CNES's JASON-1 and SPOT-5.

**United Nations**

Within the United Nations system responsibility for emergency response rests with the Resident Coordinator within the affected country.

**World Bank**

Since 1980, the World Bank has approved more than 500 operations related to disaster management, amounting to more than US$40 billion.

These include post-disaster reconstruction projects, as well as projects with components aimed at preventing and mitigating disaster impacts.

## National Organizations

In India, the role of emergency management falls to National Disaster Management Authority of India, a government agency subordinate to the Ministry of Home Affairs. Survey of India, an agency within the Ministry of Science and Technology, is also playing a role in this field, through bringing the academic knowledge and research expertise of earth scientists to the emergency management process.

Recently the Government has formed the Emergency Management and Research Institute (EMRI).

This group represents a public/private partnership, funded primarily by a large India-based computer company "Satyam Computer Services", and aimed at improving the general response of communities to emergencies, in addition to those incidents which might be described as disasters.

**Risk Identification: Early Warnings (1)**

- Observational data are needed for the study of climate variability and issue of warnings for climate-related disasters-issued from weeks to seasons in advance if adequate climate predictions are available.
- Regular assessments and authoritative statements on climate variability. Climate alert system for early warnings on pending significant climate anomalies.

**Risk Identification: Early Warnings (2)**

- WMO's World Climate Programme (WCP) is monitoring and issuing El Niño outlooks, which alerts governments to prepare to El Niño related anomalies.
- Regional Climate Outlook – important development for evaluation of seasonal forecasts.
- Forums- have become regular meetings in some regions, where NMHSs meet to discuss global climate model outputs and develop consensus seasonal forecasts for regional and local use.

**Preparedness and Emergency Management**

- Timely and accurate forecasts and warnings of natural hazards coupled with adequate local preparedness planning are fundamental requirements for disaster reduction.
- Optimal response to natural disasters requires effective coordination and cooperation between responsible agencies, institutions, officials, the media, political leaders and other players at local, national and international levels.
- WMO will support the NMHSs to establish and enhance partnerships between NMHSs and the national authorities and organizations involved in the natural disaster reduction activities to improve preparedness and emergency planning.

**Governance Support**

- Legislation and adequate normative framework are essential to implement risk management.

- Political commitment is crucial to allocate the necessary resources.
- Contributions of NMHSs need to be integrated in national disaster management plans.
- WMO is supporting NMHSs to promote natural disaster reduction and mitigation as national priority action by the Governments.

## Conclusions

1. Need for an integrated approach
    - National and regional levels
        - Role of National Meteorological and Hydrological Services
        - Cooperation across disciplines and agencies
        - Links with academic community.
    - International level
        - Between IGOs and NGOs concerned
        - Capacity building and transfer of technology activities
    - In multiple domains
        - observations
        - communications
        - data processing, etc.,
2. Need for an integrated approach
    - In multiple domains
        - observations
        - communications
        - data processing, etc.,

## What Can Vets do?

Veterinary professionals can play two major roles in emergency management cycles.

- Firstly, they can offer traditional rescue and emergency services after disasters. They can join with humanitarian relief efforts and follow up with recovery programmes; for example, to control dog populations.
- Secondly, they can get involved in the mitigation and preparedness phases. With their knowledge of the epidemiology of endemic and post disaster diseases, animal health and husbandry, nutrition and behavior.

- Vets, more than any other professionals, can make a vast contribution to improving the quality of life for both animals and their owners.

### International Strategy for Disaster Reduction

## What is Disaster Risk Reduction (Drr)?

A conceptual framework consisting of ways and means:

- To minimize vulnerabilities and disaster risks.
- To avoid (prevention) or to limit (mitigation and preparedness) the adverse impacts of natural phenomena or hazards within the context of sustainable development.

### ISDR

1. The International Decade for Natural Disaster Reduction (IDNDR, 1990-1999)
2. World Conference on Natural Disaster Reduction, held in Yokohama, Japan in 1994; "Yokohama Strategy for a Safer World: Guidelines for Natural Disaster Prevention, Preparedness and Mitigation" and its Plan of Action adopted.
3. The UN General Assembly adopted the International Strategy for Disaster Reduction (ISDR) in December 1999 to follow up on the IDNDR;
4. World Conference on Disaster Reduction took place from 18-22 January 2005, Kobe, Hyogo, Japan aimed to launch specific initiatives or partnerships to support the implementation of the ISDR as well as to facilitate networking and exchange of information between partners and organization;
5. Proposed or ongoing programmes and projects; capacity building for space technology application, weather forecast application, Regional Drought Preparedness Network for Asia (ESCAP, ISDR, UNDP, UNCCD Secretariat and ADPC (Asian Disaster Preparedness Center, Pathumthani, Thailand), GEF.

### International Strategy for Disaster Reduction

- Launched in 2000 by UN General Assembly Resolution A/54/219 as successor of the International Decade on Natural Disaster Reduction – IDNDR, 1990-1999
- The ISDR aims at building disaster resilient communities by promoting increased awareness of the importance of disaster reduction as an integral

component of sustainable development, with the goal of reducing human, social, economic & environmental losses due to natural hazards and related technological & environmental disasters.

**ISDR Bodies**

The ISDR combines the strengths of many key players through the Inter-Agency Task Force on Disaster Reduction (IATF/DR) and the Inter-Agency Secretariat of the ISDR (UN/ISDR).

1. Inter-Agency Task Force for Disaster Reduction (IATF/DR) (2 meetings/ year: April/May and Oct/Nov. in Geneva)

The IATF/DR is the principal body for the development of disaster reduction policy. It is headed by the UN Under-Secretary General for Humanitarian Affairs and consists of 25 UN, international, regional and civil society organizations. It meets twice a year in Geneva, Switzerland. Working Groups reporting to the IATF/DR bring together specialists and organisations to discuss issues of common and global relevance to disaster reduction such as climate variability, early warning, vulnerability and risk analysis, wild land fires and drought

2. Inter-Agency Secretariat of ISDR

(Headquarters in Geneva)

- Regional offices (Africa, Americas, planned: Asia, Europe)
- Partner Networks and Regional Centres (AU, NEPAD, CDERA, CEPREDENAC, CAPRADE, ADPC, ADRC, SOPAC, COE, IC/CIS...)
- National Platforms or Committees

The **UN/ISDR** is the focal point in the UN System to promote links and synergies between, and the coordination of, disaster reduction activities in the socio-economic, humanitarian and development fields, as well as to support policy integration. It serves as an international information clearinghouse on disaster reduction, developing awareness campaigns and producing articles, journals, and other publications and promotional materials related to disaster reduction.

**ISDR: Main functions**

(a) Policy & Strategy: mainstreaming risk reduction

(b) Advocacy: education, training & awareness

(c) Information Management and Networks

(d) Partnerships for Applications.

## Disaster Risk Reduction Movement–ISDR System

**Objective:** To reduce disaster risk, worldwide, Focussing on nations and communities

**The instrument :** Hyogo Framework for Action- 2005-2015

**The vehicle :** ISDR system- 'movement'

## World Conference on Disaster Reduction

Hyogo Framework for Action 2005-2015 (HFA)

### Three Strategic Goals

- The integration of disaster risk reduction into sustainable development policies and planning.
- The development and strengthening of institutions, mechanisms and capacities to build resilience to hazards.
- The systematic incorporation of risk reduction approaches into the implementation of emergency preparedness, response and recovery.

### Five priorities for action

1. Governance : ensure that disaster risk reduction is a national and local priority with strong institutional basis for implementation.

   **Key activities**

   i. National institutional and legislative frameworks

   ii. Resources

   iii. Community participation

2. Risk identification : Identify, assess and monitor disaster risks and enhance early warning

   **Key activities**

   i. National and local risk assessments

   ii. Early warning

   iii. Capacity

   iv. Regional and emerging risks.

3. Knowledge: Use of knowledge, innovation and education to build a culture of safety and resilience at all levels.

   **Key activities**

   i. Information management and exchange

   ii. Education and training

iii. Research

iv. Public awareness

4. Reducing the underlying risk factors in various sectors (environment, health, construction, etc.)
5. Strengthen disaster preparedness for effective response.

**Haiti Earthquake**

"A Partnership between the **World Bank** and the **International Strategy for Disaster Reduction** (ISDR) system to support the implementation of the Hyogo Framework for Action 2005-2015: Building the Resilience of Nations and Communities to Disasters"

**Concept and Meaning of Disaster Management**

## Definition

WHO defines Disaster as "any occurrence, that causes damage, ecological disruption, loss of human life, deterioration of health and health services, on a scale sufficient to warrant an extraordinary response from outside the affected community or area"

Disaster by landslides

Destruction by cyclone

Disaster by Tsunami

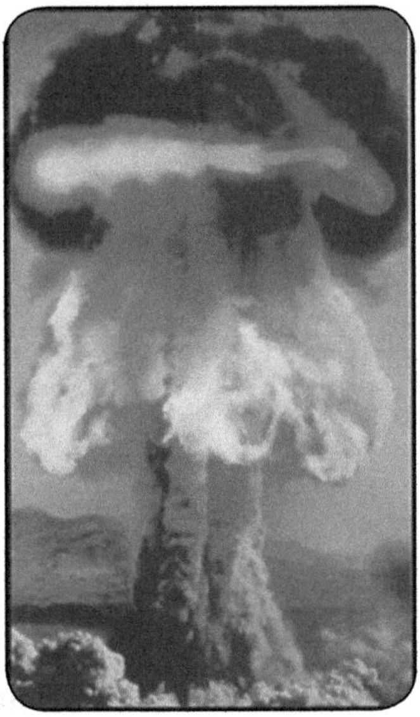

Nuclear Holocaust

**Disasters are classified in various ways**

- Natural disasters and Man made disasters
- Sudden disasters and Slow onset disasters

**Disasters include**

- Tornadoes
- Fires
- Hurricanes
- Floods / Sea Surges / Tsunamis

- Snow storms
- Earthquakes
- Landslides
- Severe air pollution (smog)
- Heat waves
- Epidemics
- Building collapse
- Toxicological accidents (e.g. release of hazardous substances)
- Nuclear accidents
- Explosions
- Civil disturbances
- Water contamination and
- Existing or anticipated food shortages

### Disasters Effects

- Disasters throughout history have had significant impact on the numbers, health status and life style of populations.
- Deaths
- Severe injuries, requiring extensive treatments
- Increased risk of communicable diseases
- Damage to the health facilities
- Damage to the water systems
- Food shortage
- Population movements.

### India's Natural Disasters Proneness

- On the basis of geographic and climatic considerations, India can be divided into 5 Zones according to its disaster proneness to natural disasters;

1. Northern mountain region including foot hills; this region is prone to strong Snow Storms leading to Land slides and strong Cold waves and also is Earthquake prone belt with violent subterranean Volcanic activity.
2. Indo-gangetic plains; heavy rains during monsoon make these plains vulnerable to Floods.
3. Deccan plateau; a Drought prone area.

4. The western desert; a Drought prone area.
5. Coastal areas; they are prone to Sea erosion, Cyclones and Tidal waves.

### India's Disaster Ridden History

- About 60% of India's land mass is prone to Earth Quakes
- Over 40 million Hectares are prone to Floods
- Nearly 3 lakh sq. km are at risk of Cyclones
- The Earth quake in Bhuj killed 14,000 people
- Cyclone in Orissa took away 10,000 lives.
- Between 1990 and 2000 an average of about 3400 people lost their lives annually.
- About 3 crore people were affected by Disasters every year.
- About 17,000 people perished by the Tsunami on 26 Dec.04.

### Vulnerable Populations

- A disaster occurring in a deserted area would be considered a natural hazard; but if it occurred in a mega city it would be recognized as a major disaster.
- Man made emergencies and another type of emergency that has to do with population vulnerability concerns technological disasters such as those of a Chemical or Radiological or Nuclear in nature. E.g. Bhopal Gas Tragedy.

### Fundamental Aspects of Disaster Management

1. Disaster response
2. Disaster Preparedness
3. Disaster Mitigation
4. Disaster Recovery.

## Response

The response phase includes the mobilization of the necessary emergency services and first responders in the disaster area. This is likely to include a first wave of core emergency services, such as firefighters, police and ambulance crews. When conducted as a military operation, it is termed Disaster Relief Operation (DRO).

They may be supported by a number of secondary emergency services, such as specialist rescue teams.

## Recovery

The aim of the recovery phase is to restore the affected area to its previous state. Recovery efforts are primarily concerned with actions that involve rebuilding destroyed property, re-employment, and the repair of other essential infrastructure. The assistance for recovery may be provided by national or international agencies and organisations.

## Mitigation

Mitigation efforts attempt to prevent hazards from developing into disasters altogether, or to reduce the effects of disasters when they occur. Mitigation is the most cost-efficient method for reducing the impact of hazards, however it is not always suitable.

Mitigation does include providing regulations regarding evacuation, sanctions against those who refuse to obey the regulations (such as mandatory evacuations), and communication of potential risks to the public.

## Preparedness

- Communication plans with easily understandable terminology and methods.
- Proper maintenance and training of emergency services, including mass human resources such as community emergency response teams.
- Development and exercise of emergency population warning methods combined with emergency shelters and evacuation plans.
- Stockpiling, inventory, and maintain disaster supplies and equipment.
- Develop organizations of trained volunteers among civilian populations.

### Prevention of Disasters

- Hurricane/Tornado/ Cyclone warning systems
- Legislation preventing building in the flood AND landslide prone areas
- Requirement of protective cellars/shelters in disaster prone areas
- A Seismic housing code for earthquake-prone area
- Strict procedural code followed to prevent Nuclear, Toxicological and Chemical disasters
- Early warning systems, and Disaster preparedness which will help to minimize morbidity, mortality and economic loss.

**Surveillance following a disaster evolves in phases**

1. Immediate Assessment
2. Short term assessment
3. Ongoing Surveillance.

## Immediate Assessment

- The object of this phase of surveillance is to obtain as much general information as possible and as quickly as possible
- **An Arial survey** may be useful in defining the geographical extent of the disaster-stricken area and in observing major damage and destruction.
- **Census data** can be examined to determine how many people previously lived in the disaster-stricken area and thus were at risk.
- **Hospitals, clinics, and morgues,** which were in operation, may be able to obtain numbers of known deaths and injuries.

## Short Term Assessment

The short-term assessment involves more systematic methods of collecting data and is likely to result in more detailed reliable information on problems, relief resources, and relief information on problems, relief resources and relief activities in progress.

### Ongoing Surveillance

- Depending on the factors above, short-term assessment may take as little as 5-6 hours or up to 3-4 days. As early as possible, relief priorities should be determined, resources ordered and full scale relief activities initiated.
- Once the short-term assessment is complete and appropriate relief is in progress, surveillance becomes an ongoing system.

### Victims and Survivors

- Almost everyone in the population is affected by a disaster. No one is untouched by it. Those who suffer damage are called victims. The victims may die or live. Those who manage to live are called survivors. These survivors can be classified as,
- Primary survivor – One who is exposed to the disaster first-hand and then survives. They are called 'survivor victims'.
- Secondary survivor – One who grieves the loss of primary victims. Example, a mother who lost her child, or a man who lost his friend.

A relief plan developed during any of the surveillance cycle may include some or all of the following activities:

- Rescue of victims
- Provision of emergency medical care
- Elimination of physical dangers (fire, gas leak etc)
- Evacuation of the population (nuclear and chemical emergencies)
- Provision of preventive and routine medical care to man and animal
- Provision of water
- Provision of food
- Provision of clothing
- Provision of shelter
- Disposal of human waste
- Control of vector born diseases
- Disposal of human and animal bodies
- Disposal of solid waste.

**International and National Organizations**

**International Association of Emergency Managers**

**Red Cross/Red Crescent**

**United Nations.**

**World Bank.**

National Disaster Management Authority of

India (NDMAI).

Emergency Management and Research

Institute (EMRI).

**Financial Arrangement in Disasters**

## Calamity Relief Fund (CRF)

- The basic responsibility for undertaking rescue, relief and rehabilitation measures in the event of natural disasters is that of the concerned State Governments.
- The role of the Central Government is supportive.

- The Department of Agriculture & Cooperation (DAC) is the nodal Department in Government of India for natural disaster management.
- The policy and arrangements for meeting relief expenditure are, by and large based on the recommendations of successive Finance Commissions.
- Margin money was allocated to each State for meeting immediate needs of expenditure on relief measures.
- If the State Govt. estimated expenditure exceeds the quantum of margin money available in the state, it has to present memorandum for Central assistance.
- An inter-ministerial Central Team was deputed to assess the quantum of central assistance to be provided to the state.
- A High Level Committee on Relief (HLCR) having representatives of all the concerned ministries considered the recommendations of the central teams extend the central assistance.

**Margin money allotted during different Finance Commission**

- Sixth FC (1974-1979) – Rs. 318 crore.
- Seventh FC (1979-1984) – extra central assistance should be limited to 5% of the Annual plan out lay of that year.
- Eighth FC (1984-1989) - Half the margin money was taken into 'account in the forecasts' of State's budgets as determined by the Finance Commissions and the remaining half was to be provided by the Center after the States exhausted the funds available with them.

**Ninth Finance Commission(1990-95)**

- Creation of separate Relief fund for each state.
- Formation of state level committee under state chief secretary to handle this fund.
- Co-ordination and monitoring by Union Ministry of Agriculture.
- Handling of calamities of rare severity by center involving additional central assistance over and above the CRF.

**Tenth Finance Commission (1995-2000)**

- It recommended creation of National Fund for Calamity Relief(NCRF) in addition to CRF.
- The Agriculture Ministry was required to issue guidelines for being

followed by the State Level Committees.

- The State Accountant Generals should then be instructed to see that only expenditure on the items approved by the Agriculture Ministry is booked under the Head "Natural Calamities".

**National Fund for Calamity Relief**

- Deals with calamities of 'rare severity' requiring central intervention
- The size of the fund was to be Rs. 700 crore, to be built up over the period 1995-2000, with an initial corpus of Rs. 200 crore to which the Centre would contribute Rs. 150 crore and the States Rs. 50 crore in the proportion of 75:25.
- In addition, for each of the five years from 1995-96 to 1999-2000 the contributions of the Centre and the States was to be Rs. 75 crore and Rs. 25 crore respectively.

## National Calamity Relief Fund Committee (NCRC)

- This is a subcommittee of the National Development Council headed by
  - The Union Agriculture Minister and
  - Deputy Chairman Planning Commission,
  - Two Union Ministers and
  - Five Chief Ministers nominated by the Prime Minister annually by rotation.

**Eleventh Finance Commission (2000-2005)**

- The CRF should be used for meeting the expenditure for providing immediate relief to the victims of cyclone, drought, earthquake, fire, flood and hailstorm.
- The release of the funds from the Centre to the CRF of each State may be done in two installments, viz. on 1st of May and 1st of November each year.
- Every State should prepare an Annual Report on natural calamities relating to the preceding financial year, and submit it to the Union Ministry of Agriculture by the 30th September every year.
- The Union Ministry of Agriculture should bring out a Report on the Natural Calamities and their Management, by 31st December every year.
- National Calamity Contingency Fund (NCCF).

**Gratuitous Relief**

| Items | Norms of assistance |
|---|---|
| Ex-Gratia payment to the families of deceased persons | Rs. 1.00 lakh per deceased |
| Ex-Gratia payment for loss of a limb or eyes. | (i) Rs. 35,000/- per person (when the disability is between 40% and 75%<br>(ii) Rs. 50,000/- per person ( when the disability is more than 75% |
| Grievous injury requiring hospitalization | Rs. 7,500 per person (more than a week). |
| | Rs.2,500/- per person (less than a week). |
| Relief for the old, infirm and destitute children. | Rs. 20/- per adult, and Rs. 15/- per child per day. |
| Loss of clothing and utensils | Rs. 1000/- per each |

**Assistance to small and marginal farmers for**

| Items | Norms of assistance |
|---|---|
| (a) Desilting of agricultural Land | Rs. 6000/- per hectare |
| (b) Removal of debris on agricultural land in hilly areas | Rs. 6000/- per hectare |
| (c) Desilting/ Restoration/ Repair of fish farms | Rs. 6000/- per hectare` |
| (d) Loss of substantial portion of land caused by landslide, avalanche, change of course of rivers. | Rs.15,000/- per hectare |
| II.<br>(a) Agriculture input subsidy where crop loss was 50% and above.<br>(b) For agriculture crops, horticulture crops and annual plantation crops<br>(c) Perennial crops | Rs. 2000/- per hectare in rain fed areas<br>Rs. 4,000/- per hectare for areas under assured irrigation.<br>Rs 6,000 per hectare for all types of perennial crops |
| Assistance to Small & Marginal sericulture farmers | Rs. 2000/- per ha. for Eri, Mulberry and Tussar<br>Rs. 2500 per ha. for Muga |

### Animal Husbandry Department- Assistance to small and marginal farmers/agricultural labourers

| | |
|---|---|
| **Milch animal**<br>Buffalo/ cow/camel / yak etc.<br>Sheep/Goat | Rs. 10,000/-<br><br>Rs. 1000/- |
| **Drought Animals:**<br>Camel/horse/ bullock, etc.<br>Calf, Donkey, and pony | <br>Rs. 10,000/-<br>Rs. 5000/- |
| **Poultry** | Rs. 30/- per bird subject to a ceiling of assistance of Rs.300/- per beneficiary household |
| Provision of fodder / feed concentrate in the cattle Camps | Large animals- Rs. 20/ per day<br>Small animals- Rs. 10/- per day |

### Assistance to Fisherman

| **Items** | **Norms of assistance** |
|---|---|
| For repair / replacement of<br><br>boats, nets – damaged or lost | Rs.2,500/- (for repair of partially damaged traditional)<br><br>Rs. 7500/- (for replacement of fully damaged) |
| Input subsidy for fish seed farm | Rs. 4,000/- per Hectare |

### Assistance for repair/ restoration of damaged houses

| **Items** | **Norms of assistance** |
|---|---|
| Fully damaged/ destroyed houses<br>Pucca house<br>Kutcha House | <br>Rs. 25,000/- per house<br>Rs. 10,000/- per house |
| Severely damaged Houses<br>Pucca House<br>Kutcha House | Rs. 5,000/- per house<br>Rs. 2,500/- per house |
| Partially Damaged Houses – both pucca/ kutcha | Rs. 1500 /- per house |
| Huts :damaged /Destroyed | Rs. 2000/- per Hut |

## District Level Funds

- Fifty percent contribution coming from the public, and rest be matching grant from the State CRF.
- The District level Relief Committee under the chairmanship of the District Collector would evolve the guidelines and norms for expenditure from the district level funds.

**Water supply in cattle camps**

- Additional cost of medicines and vaccine (calamity related requirements).
- Supply of fodder outside cattle camps.
- Movement of useful cattle to other areas.

**Extra items cover under CRF**

- Provision of emergency supply of drinking water in rural areas and urban areas.
- Provision of medicines, disinfectants, insecticides for prevention of outbreak of epidemics.
- Medical care for cattle and poultry against epidemics as a sequel to a notified natural calamity.
- Evacuation of people affected/likely to be affected.
- Hiring of boats for carrying immediate relief & saving life.
- Provision for temporary accommodation, food, clothing, medical care etc. of people affected/ evacuated (operation of relief camps).
- Air dropping of essential supplies.
- Replacement of damaged medical equipment and lost medicines of Govt. hospitals/ health centres.
- Operational cost for Ambulance Service, MobileMedical Teams and temporary dispensaries.
- Cost of clearance of debris.
- Draining off flood water in affected areas.
- Cost of search and rescue measures.
- Disposal of dead bodies/carcasses.
- Training to specialist multidisciplinary groups/ teams of the State personnel drawn from different cadres/services/ personnel involved in management of disaster in the State".
- Procurement of essential search, rescue and evacuation equipments including communication equipments.

## The Role of NGOs in Disaster Management

NGOs are defined as "private organizations which conduct and pursue activities to relieve sufferings, promote the interests of poor, provide basic social services or undertake community development".

In wider usage, the term NGO can be applied to any non profiting organization which is independent from the government. NGOs are typically value based organizations which depend, in whole or in part, on charitable donations and voluntary service. Although the NGO sector has become increasingly professional over the last two decades, principles of altruism and voluntarism remain key defining characters. NGOs range in their size and scope from large charities as CARE, OXFAM, World Vision of global fame to regional, national and community based self help groups. They include research centres, religious institutions and professional associations. Based on their functioning NGOs can be divided in two distinct categories.

Operational NGOs. Such organizations work for the betterment of humanity through practical application of their resources and abilities. They under take welfare measures, development projects and assists the governments and its agencies in crises management.

Advocacy NGOs. This type of NGOs are more focused and deals with a specific purpose with a view to defend and promote a particular cause. Commonly dealt issues are health, education and poverty. At times a no of advocacy NGOs may unite under a single operational NGO while advocating their particular cause. Physical application usually is not within the domain of such types.

Operational NGOs find their roots in masses on contrary to the other type. Their role in disaster management is of paramount importance. These can further be classified as under.

**Community Based Organizations**: These are normally membership organizations made up of a group of individuals who have joined together to further their own interests. Normally based on communal system such organizations are weak in resources and funds with prime dependence on charity and donations. However, having grass root foundations, if linked with the two types being described below, communal organizations can be very effective.

**National Organizations**: Well financed and sufficiently equipped such organizations have national objectives. They primarily focus within the boundaries of a particular country, although at times may have international links. Edhi foundation and Insar Burni trust are the glaring examples.

**International Organizations**: Normally based in developed countries such organizations operate around the world particularly the developing countries. They have a wider scope and are linked to world fame bodies as UNO and World Bank. At times they play an intermediary role between these organizations, governments and small scaled NGOs.

**Role** in October 8th Disaster. The country saw more than 160 local, regional and international NGOs responding to the disaster. They brought specialized capabilities and resources with varying means to apply them. The major contributions can be listed as under.

Augmentation and occasional replacement of local and regional administration.

Provision of mass casualty evacuation and related relief. Assistance in restoration of basic life support systems and public services. Coordinating and prioritizing the efforts of independent volunteers. Communication and sharing of information among government agencies, various private entities and the public. Specialized tasks of medication, engineering services, transportation and shelter provision.

- The support was massive and above expectation. However, the absence of a coordinated effort and the resultant incorrect application was the sore part. An in depth analysis of their working and contributions to determine their positives and negatives is therefore a must. The recent experience reveals their under mentioned strengths and weaknesses.

## Positives

**Strong Grass Root Links:** Gaining their strength from the masses these organizations are well linked in their areas of influence. Moreover, their selfless approach and unpaid working, help them gain the sympathies of people. Innovative and Adaptable. In most cases NGOs do not have a set agenda to operate. Their basic aim being to serve humanity they are capable to undertake varying nature of tasks.

**Sincerity of Purpose**: At occasions NGOs are blamed to have secondary objectives of self propagation. In certain cases it might be true, however, the basic purpose to serve humanity remains in built to any NGO. Expertise. NGOs are usually well trained and have requisite expertise to apply their resources. They have the specialized man power and technical know how to implement their objectives. Cost Effective. Charity and donations forms the base of their finances. This very system, make these outfits highly productive with almost negligible input.

## Negatives

**Limited Institutional Capacity**: In most cases the scope of NGOs particularly at national level and below does not match their organizational abilities. Their intended tasks are usually not within their own capabilities and they normally need outside assistance from the government and local establishment. Resource and Financial Constraint. Small scaled NGOs normally do not have sufficient funds and resources to manage their affairs. Absence of a regular source of income and mere dependence on donors and charity are their vulnerabilities.

**Isolated Working:** NGOs are very weak in inter communication and coordinated working, either with the government or with their fellow organizations. They have their own agenda and work with a particular mind set. In large scale disasters duplication and wastage of efforts are therefore a common doing.

**Limited Field Sustainability:** Dealing with disasters at occasions require prolonged field employment. The associated staff of NGOs are normally not permanent. They are linked to some other jobs for their regular incomes. Long term employment of NGOs for field work is therefore a problem.

Compatible Understanding: Their direction and way of working is self assessed. They usually lack understanding of the broader social and economic context. The problem arises when they have to operate in coordination with the government and its agencies. Their limited focus and inability to view the overall framework not only limits their own out put but is also a drag on others.

**The Role of Community Based Organizations in Disaster Management**

## Introduction

The rapid world population growth is likely to further boost the impact and severity of any disaster. Disaster management, as such, needs to be placed within a holistic setting to insure that each and every disaster is viewed as a shared responsibility. To this end, it is imperative to consider a number of influences, which include "economic, social, cultural, institutional, political, and even psychological factors that shape people's lives in disaster situations".

The Bam earthquake experience in Iran underlines the need for devising a comprehensive approach toward severe disasters that could occur in the future. In this endeavor, the role of communities assumes utmost importance from several perspectives. One example would be communities playing the dual role of victim-rescuer at the response phase of a severe disaster. The present paper uses empirical findings that support the notion of community engagement in disaster management. For example, one study shows a positive correlation between the people's level of education and their preparedness to deal with a possible earthquake. When it comes to interaction between communities and organisations, studies indicate that people lack comprehensive knowledge of earthquake relief organisations, such as the Red Crescent Society. Understandably, the extent of community engagement in disaster management is directly linked to the level of people's education. In addition, the level of community trust in an organisation is also associated with the level of community engagement in that organisation's activities. In essence, a broader and more inclusive definition of disaster management is essential to cover community engagement.

Severe disasters affect the entire society and communities and, as such, can be understood and dealt with through collaboration among several academic disciplines. Engaging communities in disaster management is, furthermore, practically understood within a comprehensive model of action. Consequently, integrating the findings of academic disciplines in studying severe disasters constitutes a macro level of analysis and translating these findings into a model of action is possible in a holistic paradigm. In addition, considering the advantages of the past disaster management approaches is an integral part of a holistic approach toward a 'disaster knowledgeable community'.

## Approaches to disaster management

There are four models, including the disaster-resistant community, the disaster-resilient community, sustainable development/sustainable hazards mitigation and invulnerable development concepts. Concluding that these models are incomplete, they presented the 'comprehensive vulnerability management' concept in order to provide a holistic approach to disaster management. The present paper puts forth another model called 'disaster knowledgeable community'. Three tables offer a comparison of these models. Table 1 compares the models in terms of type and phase of disasters. Table 2 compares the approaches to disaster management by highlighting the role of actors and variables. Finally, Table 3 compares the academic dimensions of the approaches, including the interest of discipline and the level of analysis.

**Table 1** Comparison of paradigms in terms of type and phase of disasters

| **Hazards** | | **Phases/ functional areas** | |
|---|---|---|---|
| A | Disaster-resistant community | Natural, technological, civil, biological | Mainly preparedness and response |
| B | Disaster-resilient community | Natural | Mitigation |
| C | Sustainable development and sustainable hazards mitigation | Natural | Recovery and mitigation to a lesser extent |
| D | Invulnerable development | Natural (especially flooding) and technological to a lesser extent | Mitigation and recovery |
| E | Comprehensive vulnerability management | Natural, technological, civil, biological | Mitigation, preparedness, response, and recovery |
| F | Disaster knowledgeable community | Natural, technological, civil, biological | Mainly preparedness and response |

The disaster-resistant community model is defined as a "means to assist communities in minimizing their vulnerability to natural hazards by maximizing the application of the principles and techniques of mitigation to their development and/or redevelopment decision-making process". The disaster-resistant community model is helpful in understanding how to face severe natural disasters; however, it has its own drawbacks. The disaster-resistant community model assumes a passive role for the community, as it is more relevant to the decision-making process than to engaging the communities. The disaster-resistant community approach is more pertinent to disciplines such as geography, engineering, and urban planning. Consequently, it is not a holistic approach to disaster management, as it ignores the contribution of many academic disciplines, such as public administration, sociology, economics, political science, anthropology and psychology.

The disaster-resilient community cannot be as easily and clearly defined as the disaster-resistant community. What is clear in the literature, however, is that the concept of resilience refers to the ability to recover normality after a disaster. The concept of resilience, moreover, emphasises reaction to natural disasters at the early stage of disaster cycle. In comparison with the disaster-resistant community concept, the concept of resilience more specifically covers the social variables. Consequently, the disaster-resilient community concept encompasses more academic disciplines like sociology, economy, anthropology and psychology. The concept is, however, mainly about natural disasters and adopts a reactive approach to disasters. The concept of resilience ignores mitigation and preparedness functions, such as community education, planning, training and exercises.

The sustainable development approach to disasters is not limited to disaster management, as it places disaster management in the wider perspective of development. The concept of sustainable development emphasises the needs of future generations while responding to the modern day development programs. The sustainable hazard mitigation concept, which is very similar to sustainable development concept, appears to be more related to disaster management in this approach. Sustainable development and sustainable hazard mitigation view disasters from a broad perspective and connect the issue of disasters to other problems. These concepts provide a wider approach to disaster in comparison with disaster-resistant community and disaster-resilient community. They are not, however, holistic because they ignore man-made disasters.

As already mentioned, Tables 1 to 3 compare the approaches to disaster management. introduce comprehensive vulnerability management as a holistic and complete approach to disaster management. This approach includes all hazards, actors, phases, and disciplines. The present paper attempts to develop another model based on lessons learned from the Bam earthquake in Iran. The proposed model is by no means claimed to be comprehensive in terms of types of hazards and phases of disaster management. Nonetheless, it further emphasises the role of community. In other words, the model proposed in this paper differs from the holistic approach of comprehensive vulnerability management. The next section provides more details about the 'disaster knowledgeable community model'.

**Developing the Disaster Knowledgeable Community model**

This section attempts to explore the concept of 'disaster knowledgeable community' by primarily examining the meanings of community and knowledge. People's engagement in disaster management is widely believed to open new windows to public decision-making. Different countries define people's engagement differently. For instance, people's engagement in Iran means involving the whole society in (responding to) disasters. In the United Kingdom and Australia, people's engagement may be defined as community engagement. The concept of community usually refers to people at the local level. For example, Buckle (2004) defines community as people at a local level who are not organised by emergency services but who have skills, resources, and capacities that allow them to provide services to people at risk in disasters. The notion of volunteerism is inherent in Buckle's definition of community engagement in disasters. Cultural differences among countries should, of course, be considered in understanding and learning from various earthquake experiences.

The complexity of transferring experience about community engagement is emphasised here. The culture of volunteerism and the sense of neighbourliness drive community engagement in Australia. A similar culture of volunteerism and a sense of neighbourliness can be observed in Iran, which also enjoys a culture of nationalism and a sense of brotherhood. The culture of nationalism suggests that engaging the community may be translated into engaging the nation. In other words, planning people's engagement in disaster management can be centralised and widely promoted throughout the country. This, however, does not mean that the operations should also be directed from the centre. A solution for Iran might be the approach of 'planning nationally and operating locally'. It is helpful to review the patterns of people's engagement in the Bam earthquake. The Bam earthquake experience indicated that community engagement in a severe disaster had different patterns. These patterns were structured in different forms, including victim-based, corroborative provinces and national media-based. The people of Bam were engaged seriously in disaster as victims and rescuers. The surviving relatives of the victims constituted the effective aid force, but lacked any organisation or training. This part of community was the core of engagement. The second circle of engagement was formed by corroborative provinces. Corroborative province refers to the communities surrounding the Kerman Province, in which the city of Bam is located. The surrounding provinces formed a circle around the core of disaster. This form of engagement was rather well organised, and trained people were engaged in the rescue, recovery, and relief operations. The national media-based engagement refers to the media, especially the radio and television, which informed the entire nation of the disaster and encouraged donations, as well as rescue, recovery, and relief aid. In the early stage of the earthquake, this engagement had an indirect impact because of distance from the core of disaster. Volunteer organisations, like the Red Crescent Society and rescue committees, collected people's donations from all across the country.

The disaster knowledgeable community model emphasises the distribution of knowledge among communities. The disaster knowledgeable community conceptualisation considers both the internal and the external dimensions of knowledge. External dimension of knowledge refers to the absorbed understanding of knowledge at the society level. The amalgamation of knower, the situation, and the environment present knowledge in a process and relational format. This sociological perspective of knowledge supports the 'disaster knowledgeable community' concept. Knowledge is widely believed to be a function of history and the interlinking of people with people, people with knowledge, and knowledge with knowledge. Consequently, the knowledge held by universities and research centres about disasters needs to be widely and thoroughly communicated to communities. Policy making about disasters necessitates considering knowledge in a broad perspective that includes social context and environment. As state, social capital is also important because the value of knowledge will increase through interaction among individuals and organisations. From a social perspective, then, knowledge is valuable only when it is understood and transferred to the society. For example, the communities' trust in organisations involved in disasters plays a major role in enriching the exchange of knowledge. Clearly, people should understand and trust the organisations to be able to cooperate with them. This understanding is also important for organisations in transferring their accumulated knowledge to communities.

Public education affords a major way to transfer knowledge to communities. Natural disasters have a low probability of occurring with a high probability of effects. Public education is essential in mitigation programs. In public education, even simple instructions play a vital role in disaster mitigation. The community education, engagement, and awareness are the most important factors in improving flood warnings in Australia. The different studies shows a positive correlation between the people's level of education and their preparedness for earthquake. The study also found that people's knowledge about organisations related to earthquake, such as the Red Crescent Society, was very low. Understandably, the level of community engagement in disaster management is associated with the level of public education. Public education needs to be designed in a progressive way in which appropriate feedback from the communities boosts the effectiveness and efficiency of education. In addition to public education, specific knowledge improvement methods are required for elites in any community. For example, complex approaches such as 'progressive discourse' and 'perspective taking and perspective making' should be considered as complementary methods for key players that have higher education.

**The Model of Disaster Knowledgeable Community in Practice**

The 'Disaster knowledgeable community' concept is introduced in this paper as an appropriate approach or model for the Iranian society. Developing a comprehensive theoretical model may create confusion for practitioners and communities. As the emergency management practitioners and community leaders may not always view the post-earthquake action in a wider framework. Apparently, the 'disaster knowledgeable community' model needs explanation to be translated into action. The metaphor of waves is used here to bridge the gap between the theory expounded in relevant literature and actual translation of the theory into practice. Observations of the early stage of the Bam earthquake constitute the practical experience leading to the metaphor of waves. There are several post disaster waves: physical, social, economic, political, and medical. 'Physical wave' is a force that not only destroys properties but also moves the other waves. The physical wave is sometimes known as the disaster itself, particularly in natural disasters, such as earthquakes and floods. Evidently, controlling the physical disaster wave in Iran could prevent the other disaster waves from being set in motion.

'Social wave' refers to the force that damages the structures and functions of a community's social order. For example, families as solid cells of community do not function normally. Specific social groups, such as women, children, the elderly and the handicapped need special attention, and their numbers increase suddenly. The majority of disaster preparation plans are devised with the ordinary citizens in mind, while children, the disabled, pregnant women, and people with special needs are ignored. They suggest including these groups in mitigation programs. Maintaining communication is very important in disasters. The Bam experience proved the vulnerability of public communication systems, such as telephone lines, to severe disasters. Developing a limited personal communication system would be very helpful in practice. This would be a technology providing effective communication service for a small group of people, such as members of a family, in crisis situations. The system should function even without electricity to connect members of a group or a family and also link any small group with the wider public systems.

'Economic wave' disturbs the normal and ordinary economic life. In this wave, distribution and supply of goods and services comes to a halt, losing its normality. Early response to this wave includes aid provided from new sources, usually outside the affected community. The main concern at this stage is equal distribution of goods and services in the short term. In the long term, funding becomes a serious problem for public officials. Damaged properties increase the level of poverty. Funding the reconstruction of properties becomes a long-term concern.

'Political wave' affects pubic officials and decision-makers at national, provincial, and local levels. This wave is sometimes very strong at the local level as it destroys local public entities and institutions. For example, almost all local officials were victims of the Bam earthquake. Consequently, officials of nearby cities were in charge of controlling the disaster outcomes. The national and provincial authorities, as well as public officials, were seriously involved in the disaster. Following the Bam earthquake, the cabinet held its meetings near Bam to facilitate communications and speed up decision making.

Perhaps the real meaning of emergency is captured in the 'medical wave'. Rescuing is the vital function of disaster response at the impact stage. The medical wave affects medical systems in a vast area of the country. The experience of the Bam earthquake proved that collecting and evacuating those injured was very difficult in a severe disaster. Almost all medical teams and hospitals neighbouring cities were involved in rescue and relief activities. In addition, many international and national medical teams were also engaged in rescue operations. Coordinating medical teams within the affected area and the rest of the country was a complex task. This wave is less manageable from the top. The normal medical system is vulnerable to severe disasters. The Bam earthquake ruined the city's hospitals and medical services. Local people in the affected area play an important role in responding to the medical disaster wave. Eshraghi underlines the need for self-organising medical teams in the early days of severe disasters. Trained individuals with required equipment can render medical services to the victims early after the disasters. These individuals can also move and form medical teams in the affected areas.

There are two waves in severe disasters — one wave, demanding medical attention, moves from the centre of the disaster, while the other wave supplies and responds to medical needs of the affected area. These two waves move in opposite directions. The meeting of these waves may or may not be managed properly. The interaction between these two waves was observed in hospitals that provided services to the victims of the Bam earthquake.

The majority of hospital personnel servicing the victims of the Bam earthquake complained of the aggressiveness and impatience of those accompanying the victims. Hospitals are designed to service a limited number of patients, not a huge number of people, including impatient relatives. Public education and public arrangements are required to deal with such situations. One way is employing volunteers who live near public organisations such as hospitals. These volunteers can help the personnel in directing people as to where they need to go. In essence, volunteers bridge the gap between organised people and unorganised communities. They sometimes work as a shield in protecting organisations from restless and unruly communities. For example, informing relatives of the patients and controlling them are serious tasks facing a hospital servicing a large number of victims. Another way is enforcing a well-designed public education system for disaster management. A well-educated community plays a major role in the responding phase of disasters. People should be aware of the vital role of hospitals in disasters. The hospital personnel should not be exhausted by having to interact with the relatives of victims. Sometimes, they have to work for days without rest. The hospitals emergency programs should, therefore, be linked with community programs.

**Rationale of Community Disaster Management through Groups**

Communities need to be prepared for natural and human made disasters because these can strike anywhere regardless of location, culture and history. Local organizations are able to react immediately and stay long after agencies have come and gone. The goals of community organizing, particularly neighbors-hood based organizing, varies but generally includes forming groups, bringing about social justice, obtaining maintaining or restructuring power, developing alternatives institutions and maintaining or revitalizing neighborhoods. Communities that are well trained culturally, socially and psychologically are better prepared and more effective in responding to the aftermath of disasters.

**Importance of Community Initiatives in Disaster Risk Reduction and Management**

When the capacities of a community are recognized the solutions come from within the community itself, making them stronger and self reliant. The solutions are realistic and the community feels responsive and involved in the disaster mitigation process, this leads to more effective and sustainable mitigation that is integrated as part of development process. There is need for community capacity building that encompass consideration, that cover housing conditions and income generation while raising awareness and educating the about consequences.Sustainable development can reduce vulnerability by addressing the root causes of disasters and the lack of access to economic and political tools.

**Community Based Disaster Management (CBDM)**

Community based disaster management can be seen as risk reduction program designed primarily by and for the people in certain disaster prone areas. Disaster mitigation using government and institutional interventions alone is insufficient because they pay little attention to addressing the community dynamics, perceptions or priorities. The aim of CBDM is to reduce vulnerabilities and strengthen people's capacities to cope with hazards.A thorough assessment of a community's exposure to hazards and an analysis of their specific vulnerabilities and capacities is the basis for activities, projects and programs that can reduce disaster risks. It is important to adapt a new strategy which directly involves the vulnerable people themselves in planning and implementation of mitigation measures. A bottom-up approach is likely to receive acceptance because considered communities are the best judges of their own vulnerability and can make the best decisions regarding their well being. Because a community is involved in the whole process, their felt and real needs as well as inherent resources are considered, therefore there is a greater likelihood that problems will be addressed with appropriate interventions. People's participation is not only focused in process but on content, the community should be able to directly gain resulting from improved disaster risk management.

**Main Characteristics of Community Based Disaster Management (CBDM)**

One promising model that incorporates the principals of community mobilization and organization is community based disaster management (CBDM) Community has a central role in long term and short term disaster management. Disaster risks or vulnerability reduction is the foundation of CBDM, the primary content of disaster management activities revolves around reducing vulnerable condition and the root cause of vulnerability. To enrich the community involvement in risk reduction, it is important to first assess the risk with the help of a community.

**Role of Local Community Groups in Disaster Management**

Informal organizations are usually locally based and managed by volunteers and may provide self help or mutual aid. The inclusion of grassroots and informal organizations can improve citizens' participation in disaster responses particularly in isolated or marginalized communities. This inclusion of these organizations can be empowering and improve access to services for such population.

**Role of Social Workers in Community Disaster Management**

- Engage in public awareness campaign about disasters.
- Coordinating disaster management and development activities
- Community capacity building at the social, economic and environmental levels.
- Enhancing community preparedness for disasters and in building social capital.
- Educating people on how to mitigate the consequences of disasters during relief, recovery and reduction preventive strategies periods.
- Playing a monumental role in providing psychological support e.g. counseling for disaster survivors.
- Tracking people down for family reunions after disasters.
- Communication particularly utilizing interpersonal communication for disseminating warning signals.
- Recruiting local volunteers who are familiar with the local logistics, resource and coordination plans.
- A contingent of trained community organizers and policy advocates is the group most capable of promoting the needs of marginalized citizens who are displaced or who have returned but are living in substandard conditions.

**Training and Capacity Building**

- The effective utilization of social capital is crucial in the building of community and institutional capacities in disaster management projects. Social capital consists of social concepts as social networks, social conflicts, social cohesion, and social interactions and solidarity.
- One tool used in disaster and complex emergencies that incorporate an understanding of local community knowledge and capacity building, one such example is PRA, an action research tool that involves community members in defining and working to solve local concerns.

**Training Requirement / Training Areas**

- Training on intervention techniques, loss and grief counseling and disaster preparedness
- Disaster management
- Crisis counseling
- Resilience
- Disaster prevention and mitigation

- Conflict management
- Crisis intervention
- Stress management
- Grief bereavement counseling
- Problem analysis
- Data collection and research
- Case management
- Networking, advocacy and leadership.

**Challenges Generally Encountered By Groups**

- Inadequate resources
- Poor quality leadership
- Dependency syndrome
- Lack of inertia
- Internal conflict
- Lack of transparency
- Inadequate organizational and management capacity.
- Conflicting government and stakeholder policies especially on cost sharing, handout and technical support.
- Community groups can be used to initiate small scale enterprises by the victims of disasters in Community groups can be used by the vulnerable and disaster groups to mobilize savings and give credit to their members
- Groups can be supported to assist disaster victims in conducting funerals and assisting the orphans and vulnerable children's Government, development partners and other stake holders can establish community enterprise funds which can be channeled through groups.

**Way Forward and Recommendations**

- Groups can be used and important vehicle for disaster risk reduction and management due to their unity of purpose
- Volunteers and social workers can form groups which will be available and very useful in times of disasters
- Vulnerable communities and disaster victims can form their own groups for their psychological support, tracing the lost relatives, sharing of grief and assisting the most affected order to restore their economic power.

## Conclusion

In an attempt to develop an appropriate model of coping with disasters, the 'disaster knowledgeable community' model was proposed here based on lessons learned in the Bam earthquake. The tables that follow compare this model with other models. The conceptual development of the model was supported by empirical studies. What made the proposed model distinct from other models was the way it considered the role of society and community. Plainly, the proposed model emphasises the need for the education of communities, considering the important role society and community knowledge play in any disaster. Consequently, public education was understood as the main concern for Iranian society to cope with disasters. Several waves, including physical, social, economic, political and medical, were used to portray and translate the proposed model into action.

### Role of Central and State Administration in Disaster Management

Under the existing framework in our country, the responsibility of undertaking rescue, relief and rehabilitation measures rests with the concerned State Government. The Central Government provides financial and logistic support in the event of major disasters. A Crisis Management Committee in the State with senior representatives from the Government Department and Central agencies located in the State oversees the Disaster management (DM) actions.

At district level, District Plans are prepared in advance for implementation during a crisis with adequate powers for decision-making. A Calamity Relief Fund at the national level provides additional funds required for various actions. The Central Relief Commissioner in the Ministry of Home Affairs is the focal point at national level. Coordinates appropriate dissemination of warnings received from India Meteorological Department, Central Water Commissioner etc,. and adequate financial support. At national level, a National Emergency Management Agency (NEMA) is being established to coordinate all aspects of DM effectively.

## Disaster Prevention and Mitigation

The Yokohama message emanating from the international decade for natural disaster reduction in May, 1994 underlined the need for an emphatic shift in the strategy for disaster mitigation. It was inter alia stressed that disaster prevention, mitigation, preparedness and relief are four elements which contribute to and gain, from the implementation of the sustainable development policies. These elements alongwith environmental protection and sustainable development, are closely inter related, and it was therefore, recommended that Nations should incorporate them in their development plans and ensure efficient follow up measures at the community, sub-regional, regional, national and international levels. The Yokohama Strategy also emphasized that disaster prevention, mitigation and preparedness are better than disaster response in achieving the goals and objectives of vulnerability reduction. Disaster response alone is not sufficient as it yields only temporary results at a very high cost. Prevention and mitigation contribute to lasting improvement in safety and are essential to integrated disaster management.

**Mainstreaming Disaster Management into Development:** The Government of India have adopted mitigation and prevention as essential components of their development strategy. The Tenth Five Year Plan document has a detailed chapter on Disaster Management. The plan emphasizes the fact that development cannot be sustainable without mitigation being built into developmental process. Each State is supposed to prepare a plan scheme for disaster mitigation in accordance with the approach outlined in the plan. In brief, mitigation is being mainstreamed into developmental planning.

**Financial Arrangement:** As indicated in the earlier chapter, the Finance Commission makes recommendations with regard to devolution of funds between the Central Government and State Governments as also outlays for relief and rehabilitation. The earlier Finance Commissions were mandated to look at relief and rehabilitation. The Terms of Reference of the Twelfth Finance Commission have been changed and the Finance Commission has been mandated to look at the requirements for mitigation and prevention apart from its existing mandate of looking at relief and rehabilitation. A Memorandum has been submitted to the Twelfth Finance Commission after consultation with States. The Memorandum proposes the creating of a disaster mitigation fund, which will assist the States in taking mitigation measures like retrofitting of lifeline buildings, coastal shelterbelt plantation etc.

The Government of India have issued guidelines that where there is a shelf of projects, projects addressing mitigation will be given a priority. It has also been mandated that each project in a hazard prone area will have disaster prevention/mitigation as a term of reference and the project document has to reflect as to how the project addresses that term of reference.

**Flood Preparedness and Response:** In order to respond effectively to floods, Ministry of Home Affairs have initiated National Disaster Risk Management Programme in all the flood-prone States. Assistance is being provided to the States to draw up disaster management plans at the State, District, Block/ Taluka and Village levels. Awareness generation campaigns to sensitize the all the stakeholders on the need for flood preparedness and mitigation measures. Elected representatives and officials are being trained in flood disaster management under the programme. Bihar, Orissa, West Bengal,

Assam and Uttar Pradesh are among the 17 multi-hazard prone States where this programme is being implemented with assistance from UNDP, USAID and European Commission.

**Earthquake Risk Mitigation:** A comprehensive programme has been taken up for earthquake risk mitigation. Although, the BIS has laid down the standards for construction in the seismic zones, these were not being followed. The building construction in urban and suburban areas is regulated by the Town and Country Planning Acts and Building Regulations. In many cases, the Building regulations do not incorporate the BIS codes. Even where they do, the lack of knowledge regarding seismically safe construction among the architects and engineers as well as lack of awareness regarding their vulnerability among the population led to most of the construction in the urban/sub-urban areas being without reference to BIS standards. In the rural areas, the bulk of the housing is non-engineered construction. The mode of construction in the rural areas has also changed from mud and thatch to brick and concrete construction thereby increasing the vulnerability. The increasing population has led to settlements in vulnerable areas close to the river bed areas which are prone to liquefaction. The Government have moved to address these issues.

**National Core Group for Earthquake Risk Mitigation:** A National Core Group for Earthquake Risk Mitigation has been constituted consisting of experts in earthquake engineering and administrators. The Core Group has been assigned with the responsibility of drawing up a strategy and plan of action for mitigating the impact of earthquakes; providing advice and guidance to the States on various aspects of earthquake mitigation; developing/organizing the preparation of handbooks/pamphlets/type designs for earthquake resistant construction; working out systems for assisting the States in the seismically vulnerable zones to adopt/integrate appropriate Bureau of Indian Standards codes in their building byelaws; evolving systems for training of municipal engineers as also practicing architects and engineers in the private sector in the salient features of Bureau of Indian Standards codes and the amended byelaws; evolving a system of certification of architects/engineers for testing their knowledge of earthquake resistant construction; evolving systems for training of maso s and carry out intensive awareness generation campaigns.

**Review of building bye-laws and their adoption:** Most casualties during earthquakes are caused by the collapse of structures. Therefore structural mitigation measures are the key to make a significant impact towards earthquake safety in our country. In view of this the States in earthquake prone zones have been requested to review, and if necessary, amend their building bye-laws to incorporate the BIS seismic codes for construction in the concerned zones. Many States have initiated necessary action in this regard. An Expert Committee appointed by the Core Group on Earthquake Risk Mitigation has already submitted its report covering appropriate amendments to the existing Town & Country Planning Acts, Land Use Zoning Regulation, Development Control Regulations & Building Bylaws, which could be used by the State Governments & the local bodies there-under to upgrade the existing legal instruments. The Model Building Bylaws also cover the aspect of ensuring technical implementation of the safety aspects in all new constructions & upgrading the strength of existing structurally vulnerable constructions. To facilitate the review of existing building byelaws and adoption of the proposed amendments by the State Governments & UT administrations, discussion workshops at regional level in the country are being organized. It is expected that all planning authorities and local bodies will soon have development control regulations and building byelaws which would include multi-hazard safety provisions.

**Development and Revision of Codes**: There are Bureau of Indian Standard (BIS) codes which are relevant for multi-hazard resistant design and construction. Some of the codes need to be updated. There are some areas for which codes do not exist. An action plan has been drawn up for revision of existing codes, development of new codes and documents/commentaries, and making these codes and documents available all over the country including on-line access to these codes. An Apex committee consisting of representatives of Ministry of Consumer Affairs, BIS and MHA has been constituted to review the mechanism and process of development of codes relevant to earthquake risk mitigation and establish a protocol for revision by BIS.

**Hazard Safety Cells in States:** The States have been advised to constitute Hazard Safety Cells (HSC) headed by the Chief Engineer, State PWD with necessary engineering staff so as to establish mechanism for proper implementation of the building codes in all future Govt. constructions, and to ensures the safety of buildings and structures from various hazards. The HSCs will also be responsible for carrying out appropriate design review of all Government buildings to be constructed in the State, act as an advisory cell to the State Government on the different aspects of building safety against hazards and act as a consultant to the State Government for retrofitting of the lifeline buildings. Rajasthan, West Bengal, Delhi and Chhatisgarh have already constituted these cells and other States are in the process.

**National Programme for Capacity Building of Engineers and Architects in Earthquake Risk Mitigation:** Two National Programmes for Capacity Building in Earthquake Risk Mitigation for Engineers and Architects respectively, have been approved to assist the State Govts in building up capacities for earthquake mitigation. Under these two programmes 10,000 engineers and 10,000 architects in the States will be given training in seismically safe building designs and related techno-legal requirements. Assistance is being provided to the State/UTs to build the capacities of more than 125 State Engineering Colleges and 110 Architecture Colleges to be able to provide advisory services to the State Govts to put in place appropriate techno-legal regime, assessment of building and infrastructures and their retrofitting. These institutions will function as State Resource Institutions. Twenty-one Engineering and Architecture Institutions have been designated as National Resource Institutes to train the faculty members of selected State Engineering and Architecture colleges. 450 engineering faculty members and 250 architecture faculty members of these State Resource Institutions will be trained during the current year.

**Training of rural masons:** A programme to assist the States/UTs in training and certification of 50000 masons has been formulated in conultation with Housing and Urban Development Corporation (HUDCO) and the Ministry of Rural Development. The training module for masons to include multi-hazard resistant construction has also been prepared by an expert committee, and revised curriculum will be introduced in the vocational training programme of Ministry of Human Resource Development.

**Earthquake Engineering in Undergraduate Engineering/Architecture Curricula**: The role of engineers and architects is crucial in reducing earthquake risks by ensuring that the construction adhere to the norms of seismic safety. In view of this, the elements of earthquake engineering is being integrated into the undergraduate engineering and architecture courses. Model course curricula have been developed for adoption by various technical institutions and universities. And circulated to the Universities and Technical Institutions for integration into the under graduate curriculum. Ministry of Home Affairs is working with All India Council of Technical Education (AICTE) and Council of Architecture (COA) for 20introduction of revised curricula for engineering and architecture course from 2005-2006.

**Retrofitting of Lifeline buildings:** While these mitigation measures will take care of the new constructions, the problem of unsafe existing building stock would still remain. It will not be possible to address the entire existing building stock, therefore the life line buildings like hospitals, schools or buildings where people congregate like cinema halls, multi-storied apartments are being focussed on. The States have been advised to have these buildings assessed and where necessary retrofitted. The Ministries of Civil Aviation, Railways,

Telecommunication, Power and Health and Family Welfare have been advised to take necessary action for detailed evaluation and retrofitting of lifeline buildings located in seismically vulnerable zones so as to ensure that they comply with BIS norms, Action plan have been drawn up by these Ministries for detailed vulnerability analysis and retrofitting/ strengthening of buildings and structures. The Ministry of Finance have been requested to advise the financial institutions to give loans for retrofitting on easy terms. Accordingly the Ministry of Finance had advised Reserve Bank of India to issue suitable instructions to all the Banks and Financial Institutions to see that BIS codes/ bye laws are scrupulously followed while financing/refinancing construction activities in seismically vulnerable zones.

**National Earthquake Risk Mitigation Project:** An Earthquake Mitigation Project has been drawn up, with an estimated cost of Rs.1132 crore. The project has been given in-principle clearance by the Planning Commission. The programme includes detailed evaluation and retrofitting of lifeline buildings such as hospitals, schools, water and power supply units, telecommunication buildings, airports/airport control towers, railway stations, bus stands and important administrative buildings in the States/UTs in seismic zones IV and V. The programme also includes training of masons in earthquake resistant constructions, as well as, assistance to the State Governments to put in place an appropriate techno legal regime.

**Accelerated Urban Earthquake Vulnerability Reduction Programme:** An accelerated urban earthquake vulnerability reduction programme has been taken up in 38 cities in seismic zones III, IV & V with population of half a million and above. These cities are Dehradun, Delhi, Jamnagar, Rajkot, Bhavnagar, Surat, Greater Mumbai, Bhiwandi, Nasik, Pune, Bhubaneswar, Cuttack, Chennai, Patna, Asansol, Guwahati, Vadodara, Koimbatore, Ahmedabad, Agara, Varanasi, Bareily, Meerut, Lucknow, Kanpur, Kolkatta, Srinagar, Jammu, Indore, Jabalpur, Amritsar, Jalandhar, Vijayawada, Dhanbad, Mangalore, Kochi, Kozhikod and Trivandrum. 474 Orientation programmes have been organized for senior officers and representatives of the local planning and development bodies to sensitize them on earthquake preparedness and mitigation measures. Training programmes have been organized for engineers and architects to impart knowledge about seismically safe construction and implementation of BIS norms. So far 1088 engineers and 825 architects have been trained. For enhanced school safety, education programmes have been organized in schools, colleges and other educational institutions. About 370 educational institutions have been visited by the earthquake disaster management specialist in these cities. This programme will be further extended to 166 earthquake prone districts in seismic zones

IV & V. Awareness generation programmes, community and neighbourhood Organization s have been started in these cities. These cities are also being assisted to review and amend their building bye-laws to incorporate multi hazard safety provisions. City Disaster Management Plans are being developed under the project. Nine Cities have prepared city Disaster Management Plans so far.

**Mainstreaming Mitigation in Rural Development Schemes:** Rural housing and community assets for vulnerable sections of the population are created on a fairly large scale by the Ministry of Rural Development under the Indira Awas Yojna(IAY) and Sampooran Grameen Rojgar Yojna(SGRY). About 250 thousand small but compact housing units are constructed every year, besides community assets such as community centres, recreation centres, anganwadi centres etc. Technology support is provided by about two hundred rural housing centres spread over the entire country. The Ministry of Home Affairs is working with the Ministry of Rural Development for changing the guidelines so that the houses constructed under IAY or school buildings/ community buildings constructed under SGRY are earthquake/cyclone/flood resistant; as also that the schemes addressing mitigation are given priority under SGRY. Ministry of Rural Development are carrying out an exercise for this purpose. This initiative is expected to go a long way in popularization of seismically safe construction at village/block level.

**Core Group on Cyclone Mitigation:** A National Core Group on Cyclone Monitoring & Mitigation has been constituted. Experts from Indian Meteorological Department, National Centre for Medium Range Weather Forecasting, Central Water Commission, National Remote Sensing Agency and Indian Space Research Organisation have been made the Members of the Core Group, besides administrators from the relevant Ministries/Departments and State Governments vulnerable to cyclones. The Group has been assigned the responsibility of looking at warning protocols for cyclones; coordination mechanism between different Central and State Ministries / Departments / Organisations; mechanism for dissemination of warning to the local people and; cyclone mitigation measures required to be taken for the coastal States. The Group will also suggest short-term and long-term measures on technology up-gradation. The cyclone warning formats have been revised to ensure that the warning is more meaningful to the community at risk. A project has been taken up with the United States for upgradation of models for cyclone track prediction.

**National Cyclone Mitigation Project:** A project for Cyclone Mitigation (estimated cost Rs.1050 crore) has been drawn up in consultation with the cyclone prone States. This project envisages construction of cyclone shelters, coastal shelter belt plantation in areas which are prone to storm surges, strengthening of warning systems, training and education etc. This project has also been given inprinciple clearance by the Planning Commission and is being taken up with World Bank assistance.

**Landslide Hazard Mitigation:** A National Core Group has been constituted under the Chairmanship of Secretary, Border Management and comprising of Secretary, Department of Science and Technology, Secretary, Road Transport & Highways, and the Heads of Geological Survey of India and National Remote Sensing Agency for drawing up a strategy and plan of action for mitigating the impact of landslides, provide advise and guidance to the State Governments on various aspects of landslide mitigation, monitor the activities relating to landslide mitigation including landslide hazard zonation and to evolve early warning systems and protocols for landslides/landslide risk reduction. The Government have designated Geological Survey of India (GSI) as the nodal agency responsible for coordinating/undertaking geological studies, landslides hazard zoantion, monitoring landslides/avalanches, studying the factors responsible and suggesting precautionary and preventing measures. The States/UTs have been requested to share the list of habitations close to landslide prone areas in order to supplement GSI's on going assessment of such areas based on the Survey of India's Toposheet and their existing data dbase on landslide for the purpose of landslide hazard zonation being carried out by them. A national strategy for mitigating landslide hazard in the county is being drawn up in consultation with all the agencies concerned.

**Disaster Risk Management Programme**: A Disaster Risk Management Programme has been taken up in 169 districts in 17 multi-hazard prone States with the assistance from UNDP, USAID and European Union. These States are Assam, Arunachal Pradehs, Bihar, Delhi, Gujarat, Maharashtra, Meghalaya, Mizoram, Manipur, Nalaland, Orissa, Sikkim, Tamil Nadu, Tripura, Uttar Pradesh, Uttaranchal and West Bengal, Under this project, the States are being assisted to draw up State, district and Block level disaster management plans; village disaster management plans are being developed in conjunction with the Panchayati Raj Institutions and disaster management teams consisting of village volunteers are being trained in preparedness and response functions such as search and rescue, first aid, relief coordination, shelter management etc. States and District level multi-hazard resistant Emergency Operation Centres (EOCs) are also being set up under the programme. Equipment needs for district and State Emergency Operation Centres have been identified by the State nodal agencies and equipment is being provided to equip these EOCs. Orientation training of masons, engineers and architects in disaster resistant technologies have been initiated in these districts and construction of model demonstration buildings will be started soon.

Under this programme Disaster Management Plans have been prepared for 8643 villages, 1046 Gram Panchayat, 188 blocks and 82 districts. More than 29000 elected representatives of Panchayati Raj Institutions have already been trained, besides imparting training to members of voluntary organizations. About 18000 Government functionaries have been trained in disaster mitigation and preparedness at different levels. 865 engineers and 425 architects have been trained under this programme in vulnerability assessment and retrofitting of lifeline buildings. 600 master trainers and 1200 teachers have already been trained in different districts in disaster preparedness and mitigation. Disaster Management Committees consisting of elected representatives, civil society members, Civil Defence volunteers and Government functionaries have been constituted at all levels including village/urban local body/ward levels. Disaster Management Teams have been constituted in villages and are being imparted training in basic functions of first aid, rescue, evacuation and related issues. The thrust of the programme is to build up capabilities of the community since the community is invariably the first responder. Capacity building of the community has been very helpful even in normal situations when isolated instances of drowning, burns etc. take place. With the creation of awareness generation on disaster mitigation, the community will be able to function as a well-knit unit in case of any emergency. Mock drills are carried out from time to time under the close supervision of Disaster Management Committees. The Disaster Management Committees and Disaster Management Teams have been established by notifications issued by the State Governments which will ensure that the entire system is institutionalized and does not disintegrate after the conclusion of the programme. The key points being stressed under this programme are the need to ensure sustainability of the programme, development of training modules; manuals and codes, focused attention to awareness generation campaigns; institutionalization of disaster management committees and disaster management teams, disaster management plans and mock-drills and establishment of techno-legal regimes.

**Human Resource Development:** Human Resource Development at all levels is critical to institutionalization of disaster mitigation strategy. The National Centre for Disaster Management at the national level has been upgraded and designated as the National Institute of Disaster Management. It is being developed as a Regional Centre of Excellence in Asia. The National Institute of Disaster Management will develop training modules at different levels, undertake training of trainers and organize training programmes for planners, administrators and command functionaries. Besides, the other functions assigned to the National Institute of Disaster Management include development of exhaustive National level information base on disaster management policies, prevention mechanisms, mitigation measures; and providing consultancy to various States in strengthening their disaster management systems and capacities as well as preparation of disaster management plans and strategies for hazard mitigation and disaster response. It has been decided to incorporate elements of disaster management in the training curricula of Civil Services. For the three All India Services (IAS, IPS and Indian Forest Service), training curricula have already been drawn up and integrated into the training curricula of these All India Services with effect from 2004-2005. For other Civil Services at the national and state levels, training modules are being developed to be included from the next year.

**NDM cells in Administrative Training Institutes:** Disaster Management faculties have already been created in 29 State level training institutes located in 28 States. These faculties are being directly supported by the Ministry of Home Affairs. The State Training Institutions take up several focused training programmes for different target groups within the State. The Disaster Management faculties in these Institutes are being further strengthened so as to enable them to develop as Institutes of Excellence for a specific disaster. Assistance to the State level training institutes will be provided by the National Institute of Disaster Management in the development of training/capsules training modules for different functionaries at different levels.

**Awareness generation:** Recognizng that awareness about vulnerabilities is a sine qua non for inducing a mindset of disaster prevention, mitigation and preparedness, the Government has initiated a nation-wide awareness generation campaign as part of its overall disaster risk management strategy. In order to devise an effective and holistic campaign, a steering committee for mass media campaign has been constituted at the national level with due representation of experts from diverse streams of communication. The Committee has formulated a campaign strategy aimed at changing peoples' perception of natural hazards and has consulted the agencies and experts associated with advertising and media to instill a culture of safety against natural hazards.

Apart from the use of print and electronic media, it is proposed to utilize places with high public visibility viz. hospitals, schools, railway stations and bus terminals, airports and post offices, commercial complexes and municipality offices etc. to make people aware of their vulnerabilities and promote creation of a safe living environment.

A novel method being tried is the use of government stationery viz. postal letters, bank stationery, railway tickets, airline boarding cards and tickets etc. for disseminating the message of disaster risk reduction. Slogans and messages for this purpose have already been developed and have been communicated to concerned Ministries/agencies for printing and dissemination. The mass media campaign will help build the knowledge, attitude and skills of the people in vulnerability reduction and sustainable disaster risk management measures.

**Disaster Awareness in School Curriculum:** Disaster management as a subject in Social Sciences has been introduced in the school curriculum for Class VIII & IX. The Central Board of Secondary Education (CBSE) which has introduced the curriculum runs a very large number of schools throughout the country and the course curriculum is invariably followed by the State Boards of Secondary Education. Teachers are being trained to teach disaster management Syllabus for Class X is being finalized and will be introduced in the course curriculum soon. The State Governments have been advised to take similar steps vis-à-vis their school boards. Several States Governments have already introduced the same curriculum in Class VIII. Ministry is working with the Council of Boardof School Education (COBSE) to facilitate inclusion of disaster management in public education in all 39 School Boards in the country.

**Information, Education and Communication:** In order to assist the State Governments in capacity building and awareness generation activities and to learn from past experiences including sharing of best practices, the Ministry of Home Affairs has compiled/prepared a set of resource materials developed by various organisations/institutions to be replicated and disseminated by State Governments based on their vulnerabilities after translating it into the local languages. The voluminous material which runs into about 10000 pages has been divided into 4 broad sections in 7 volumes. These sections cover planning to cope with disasters; education and training; construction toolkit; and information, education and communication toolkit including multi-media resources on disaster mitigation and preparedness. The Planning section contains material for analyzing a community's risk, development of Preparedness. Mitigation and disaster management plans, coordinating available resources and implementing measures for risk reduction. Model bye-laws, DM Policy, Act and model health sector plan have also been included. Education and Training includes material for capacity building and upgradation of skills of policy makers, administrators, trainers, engineers etc. in planning for and mitigating against natural disasters. Basic and detailed training modules in disaster preparedness have been incorporated along with training methodologies for trainers, for community preparedness and manuals for training at district, block, panchayat and village levels. For creating a disaster-resistant building environment, the Construction Toolkit addresses the issue of seismic resistant construction and retrofitting of existing buildings. BIS Codes, manuals and guidelines for RCC, Masonry and other construction methodologies as also for repair and retrofitting of masonry and low-rise buildings have been included.

The IEC material seeks to generate awareness to induce mitigation and preparedness measures for risk reduction. Material and strategies used by various States and international organizations, including tips on different hazards, have been incorporated along with multi-media CDs on disasters. The material has been disseminated to all the State Governments/UT Administrations with the request to have the relevant material, based on the vulnerability of each district, culled out, translated into local languages and disseminate widely down to the village level.

## The administrative response mechanism

### Central

The Central Government, with its resources, physical and financial provides the needed help and assistance to buttress relief efforts in the wake of major National Disaster (ND).

The dimensions of the response at the level of Central Government are determined in accordance with the existing policy of financing the relief expenditure and keeping in view the factors like:

i. The gravity of a natural calamity,
ii. The scale of the relief operation necessary, and
iii. The requirements of Central assistance for augmenting the financial resources at the disposal of the State Government.

The Dept of Agriculture and Cooperation (DAC) in the Agriculture Ministry is the nodal Department for all matters concerning ND relief at the Centre. In DAC, the Relief Commissioner functions as nodal officer to coordinate relief operations for all ND. The central relief commissioner monitors the developments and provides the necessary feedback, through the Agriculture Secretary to the Agriculture Minister, PM and the Cabinet. Various other committees working at the national level for the disaster management are the following:

**Cabinet Committee:** Effective implementation of relief measures

**National Crisis Management Committee (NCMC)**

**Crisis Management Group (CMG):** Chairman- Central Relief Commissioner.

### State administration

The State Government are autonomous in organising relief operations in the event of ND and in the long-term preparedness (the Central Government only supplements the efforts of the State Government). The States have Relief Commissioners who are in-charge of the relief measures in the wake of natural disasters in their respective States. The Chief Secretary is the head of the State Administration. At the level of the State Government ND are usually the responsibilities of the Revenue Dept or the Relief Department.

**State crisis management group**

Chairman- Chief Secretary/Relief Commissioner

This group comprises Senior Officers from the Dept Revenue/Relief, Home. Civil Supplies, Power, Irrigation, Water Supply, Panchayat (Local Self-Government), Agriculture, Forests, Rural Development, Health Planning, Public works and Finance. The SCMG is required to take into consideration the infrastructure and guidance received, from Government of India and formulates actions plans for dealing with different ND. It is also the duty of the Relief Commissioner of the State to establish *an* emergency operation Centre as soon as a disaster situation develops.

## District administration

States are further divided into districts, each headed by the District Collector (District Magistrate or Deputy Commissioner). The Collector exercises coordinating and supervisory powers over functionaries of all the Departments at the District level. "Local authority" includes panchayati raj institutions, municipalities, a district board, cantonment board, town planning authority or Zila Parishad or any other authority, which renders essential services within a specified local area

A District is sub-divided into sub-divisions and *Tehsils* or *Talukas*.

The head of a sub- division is called the Sub-Division Officer (SDO)

The head of a *Tehsils* known as the *Tehsildar (Tulukdar* or *Mamlatdar* in some States).

When a disaster occur, the entire machinery of the District, including officers of technical and other dept, swings into action and maintains almost continues contact with each village in the disaster threatened area. \

The various measures undertaken by the District Administration area are as follows:

**Contingency Plans** : At the district level, the disaster relief plans provide specific tasks for their implementation in respect of areas in relation to different types of disasters.

**District Relief Committee** : Includes local legislators and members of parliament.

**District Control Room** : In case of ND for day to day monitoring of the rescue and relief operations on a continuing basis.

## The Disaster Management Act, 2005

- The Disaster Management Act, 2005 was enacted on 26th December, 2005.
- This will permit the States also to have their own legislation on disaster management.

## Salient features of the DM Act - NDMA

- National Disaster Management Authority (NDMA) under the Prime Minister with nine more members for laying down the policies, plans and guidelines for disaster management.
- Advisory Committee consisting of experts in the field of disaster management.
- The Authority will be assisted by a National Executive Committee (NEC) of Secretaries to Central Government.
- NEC shall prepare a National Disaster Management Plan in consultation with State Governments.
- National Plan to include measures for prevention and mitigation, integration of mitigation measures in the development plans, and preparedness and capacity building to respond effectively.
- The National Authority to recommend guidelines for the minimum standards of relief.
- State Disaster Management Authority (SDMA) to be chaired by Chief Minister.
- One of the members may be designated as the Vice-Chairperson of the State Authority by the Chief Minister.
- The State Authority may constitute an Advisory Committee of experts.
- The State Authority shall be responsible for laying down the policies and plans for disaster management in the State.
- The State Authority shall recommend guidelines for providing minimum standards of relief.
- The State Authority will be assisted by the State Executive Committee.
- Salient features of the DM Act - DDMA.
- The State Government shall establish a District Disaster Management Authority (DDMA) in each district.
- The District Authority will be headed by District Magistrate with seven more members.

- The District Authority shall act as the district planning, coordinating and implementing body for disaster management.

### DM Act – Local Authority

- The Local Authority shall ensure training of its officers and employees and maintenance of resources so as to be readily available for use in the event of a disaster.
- It shall also ensure that all construction projects under it conform to the standards and specifications laid down.
- It shall carry out relief, rehabilitation and reconstruction activities in the affected area within its jurisdiction.

### DM Act – Funds

- National Disaster Response Fund by Central Government and grants provided by any person/institution.
- National Disaster Mitigation Fund for mitigation projects.
- The State Government to establish Disaster Response fund and Disaster Mitigation Fund at State and District Levels.
- Every Ministry/Department of Central and State Governments to make provision for funds to carry out activities set out in its disaster management plan.

**Disaster Management Teams (DMT)**

| | | |
|---|---|---|
| Early warning team | Shelter team | Resoue and evacuation team |
| Counseling | Relief and coordination team | Water and sanitation team |
| Carcasses disposal | Damage assessment | Medical and Firstaid team |

**DMTs comprise of groups of women and men volunteers assigned with a specific task for which they receive training and SOPs.**

**Government of India: Nodal Ministries / Department for Disaster Management**

| Disasters | Nodal Ministries |
|---|---|
| Natural Disasters | Agriculture |
| Air Accidents | Civil Aviation |
| Civil Strife | Home Affairs |
| Railway Accidents | Railways |
| Chemical Disasters | Environment |
| Biological Disasters | Health & family Welfare |
| Nuclear Accident | Atomic Energy |

## External Assistance -Policy

- No formal appeal for external assistance made for relief
- External assistance, if offered as solidarity accepted with gratitude
- Gujarat earthquake- international response overwhelming
- Bi-lateral agreements suggested by some countries for emergency response.

## Role of Armed Forces in Disaster Management

### Role of armed forces

- Disasters have always co-existed with civilization.
- The United Nations defined Disasters as …
- 'A serious disruption of the functioning of a community or a society causing widespread human, material, economic and environmental losses which exceed the ability of the affect community / society to cope using its own resources.
- After capacity building of the community as such, use of Armed forces, Air force, Paramilitary forces etc. should always be the last resort thereafter
- The Indian Armed Forces are supposed to be called upon to intervene and take on specific tasks only when the situation is beyond the capability of civil administration.
- In practice, the Armed Forces are the core of the government's response capacity and tend to be the first responders of the Government of India in a major disaster.
- Due to their ability to organize action in adverse ground.
- Circumstances, speed of operational response and the resources and capabilities at their disposal, the Armed Forces have historically played a

major role in emergency support functions such as communications, search and rescue operations, health and medical facilities, transportation, power, food and civil supplies, public works and engineering, especially in the immediate aftermath of disaster.

- Disaster management plans should incorporate the role expected of them so that the procedure for deploying them is smooth and quick.

## Role and Response of A separate Armed Force

The development oriented civil administration is presently not well equipped for undertaking large scale disaster response activities in the event of major and wide spread disasters. The Indian Armed Forces are one of the most dedicated, professional and modernized armed forces in the world. They have made rapid strides in technology development.

The Armed Forces and other specialized forces have to be mandated to play an important role in disaster rescue and response operations. It also indicates the necessary guidelines to the civil authorities while utilizing the services of the Armed Forces personal and various measures to ensure greater co-ordination and enhance efficiency during disaster response operations.

### International humanitarian assistance by the military

The year 2005 saw a considerable increase in the involvement by the military in international relief assistance in natural disasters, in particular in the Indian Ocean Earthquake and Tsunami as well as the South Asia Earthquake.

### Disaster Response and Role of Armed Forces, Para-Military and Other Specialized Forces

Disaster Response Management is a Multi-Agency function coordinated at a nodal point for effective delivery of relief to the victims of a disaster. The capability of an affected community is required to be reinforced by the Civil Administration who looks for a cadre of specialists, trained, disciplined and dedicated personnel who can render relief and response services in best of the manner in worst of the situations. The armed forces and central paramilitary forces are found to be the most suited for such situations.

### Armed and Para Military Forces

- The Armed Forces/Central Para Military Forces have traditionally been always responding to the need to render yeomen service to the affected communities.
- The effectiveness of disaster response largely depends on the swift alacrity to which the response and relief measures are mounted.

- A trigger mechanism for response, which demands alertness and being active all times are considered to be the essential elements.
- Armed Forces and Central Para Military Forces who meet these requirements are called upon to assist the civil administration in evacuation and shifting of people to the safer places, rescue of stranded people, setting up of relief camps, distribution of essential commodities and providing other logistical support such as restoration of communication, road and bridges among other things.

## Role of Government in Assisting Armed Forces

- The Central Government has invariably deployed the Air Force helicopter/ Army boats, Army columns, Central Para Military Forces and Medical Teams from the Armed Forces to assist the affected States in rescue and relief operations.
- Military aircrafts have always been used in transportation of essential commodities from The Government of India have also deployed Naval ships, military aircrafts, mobile hospitals etc. to render assistance to the neighboring countries hit by natural calamities.
- Prompt mobilization of essential commodities and other resources for disaster response has been forte of Armed Forces/Central Para Military Forces. far of places in short span of time.
- For the reasons stated above, whether it was devastating Bhuj earthquake of26th January 2001 or Tsunami of December 26th, 2004.
- ARMED Forces/Central Para Military Forces were the first one to respond to the situations and assist the civil administration in providing succor to the affected people.
- Realizing the importance of service rendered by the Armed Forces/Central Para Military Forces, the Government of India has decided to set up National Disaster Response Force (NDRF) consisting of 8 battalions of Central Police Forces.
- There will be a total of 144 specialist response teams consisting of 45 personnel each.
- 72 of these 144 specialist response teams will also be trained and equipped for responding to nuclear, biological and chemical related emergencies.
- One team in each battalion will also be trained in deep sea diving for the purpose of search and rescue during floods and cyclones.

## Role of Armed Forces

- Primary role –to preserve national interest and nations strategic interest.
- Secondary role-to assist civil authorities in handling internal threats, maintain essential service.
- There presence in underdeveloped areas helps in contributing where govt. Relief mechanism is weak.

**Management of Disaster by Armed Forces**

- Disaster Management Cycle
- Disaster
- Impact
- Response
- Rehabilitation
- Reconstruction
- Development
- PreventionMitigation
- Preparedness.

**Various task forces involved**

- These task forces (DMTs) are to be trained by the concerned Government line departments.
- The trainers from each line department will show their present skills through the training programmes meant to train the task forces.
- The patrolling group for example is trained by the police and civil defence on protection/vigilance of villages during disaster as well as non-disaster situations.
- The warning group again is trained by revenue and block officials to use their intelligence to gather warning information on impending disasters and effectively disseminate the same for protection of the community.
- The first aid group again is trained by the local medical officers to handle immediate medical emergencies till specialized medical attention arrives.

**Assistance Provided**

- Providing of infrastructure for support and control.
- Providing medical facilities.

- Transportation of relief materials.
- Setting up of relief camps.
- Construction of roads and bridges.
- Shifting animals and humans to safer places.
- Public health, sanitation, clean drinking water.
- Disposal of explosives, prevention of epidemic outbreak.
- Nuclear, biological, chemical disaster response.
- Armed forces will continue to be the primary respondent in future calamities provided the government takes efficient steps in developing the system.
- It is very important that armed forces formation /unit are aware of the modification required to response mechanism in accordance with the proposed system.

**Role of Police in Disaster Management**

Though there are many different types of disasters—both man-made and natural—the response of the police to these events for the most part is the same. Man-made disasters, such as bombs and arson, cause a sense of vulnerability. Natural disasters, such as hurricanes, floods, tornadoes and fires, all cause specific damage and chaos. A strong police presence in both situations can help ease victims' fears and help prevent others from taking advantage of the disaster situation.

**Crowd Control**

1. Disaster situations draw in crowds. There will be some people hoping for a glimpse of the unfolding drama. Family members and friends of the victims will be show up, hoping to glean information about their loved ones. The people involved in the situation will also be milling around, sometimes while injured or in shock. The police will cordon off areas and work to keep crowds under control.

**Public Safety**

2. Officers might go from house to house searching for the injured or needy. They can offer transportation, emergency medical care, and be a bridge between citizens and rescue personnel. They can check the credentials to see if someone really needs to be in the area. They can warn people when electric wires are on the ground, when dangerous pests are lurking around or when unstable people are nearby.

**Directing Traffic**

3. Many disasters wipe out infrastructures such as electricity, making an unsafe situation for both traffic and pedestrians. The police can close unsafe roads where downed wires, trees or flood situations might make travel unsafe. They can direct citizens through non-working traffic lights. They can re-route random traffic to safer roads and try to keep out all unnecessary traffic away. They can put roadblocks in the areas where the crisis is still underway.

**Organizing Search Teams**

4. Disaster situations often lead to family members being separated from each other. Elderly and single people are at risk if they have no one to check on them. If these citizens randomly wander around, chaos can result. The police can set up search teams and put together systems where loved ones can check on each other. They can set up command centers where the victims and family can be reunited. They can also work with emergency personnel to list the various medical facilities used for treating sick or injured people.

**Looters**

5. Unfortunately, there are always those who will take advantage of a chaotic situation. When people are evacuated from their homes or neighborhoods, houses are left unsupervised and opportunities to commit crime can be rampant. Police presence can help to ensure that looting doesn't happen. When looting does occur, the police will be ready to apprehend and arrest the suspects.

**Major Accident Hazardous Industries**

- M/s Jindal Praxiar Oxygen Company Limited, (Toranagallu PS)
- M/s JSW Steel Limited, (Toranagallu PS)
- M/s Bellary Oxygen Company Limited, (Toranagallu PS).

**Potentially Hazardous Industries**

- M/s JSW Energy Limited, (Toranagallu PS)
- M/s Monsanto India Limited, Sirivar Village, (Bellary Rural PS)
- M/s United Galva Private Limited, Mundargi Industrial Area, (Bellary Rural PS)
- M/s Pampasara Distillery Limited, Hospet. (Chitwadigi PS)
- M/s Bellary Thermal Power Station, (Kudithini PS)
- Hazardous Industries, Bellary

- Preparedness.
- Communication — Landline
  - Wireless Network
  - Mobile Network
- Mobilization of resources — Expertise from Private & Government employees.
- Evacuation — Use of vehicles to shift affected people to safer places.
- Traffic regulations — Barricading
  - Posting of men to regulate traffic
- First aid and Treatment —
  - Alert the Hospitals.
  - Arrange Transport (ambulances & other vehicles).
  - Use of megaphones fitted to Police Vehicles to inform about — Help Centers.
  - Hospitals
  - Casualties etc.
- Identification of the deceased — Use of advance technologies such as "CDR Analysis Software" to & trace the phone number and e-mail ID.

## Communication Plan

The District Control Room and other eight (8) wireless REPEATERS will transmit and receive messages in connection with the disaster and convey to the concerned. A DEDICATED LINE can be opened if the need arises. PI (W) Bellary will be responsible for effective functioning of communication system.

Apart from the strong wireless & landline network, every Police Station has been provided with mobile phones with CUG plans carried by SHOs and supervisory officers are accessible round the clock. These mobile numbers are published in media for information of general public.

## Infrastructure with Police

1. Vehicles

| | |
|---|---|
| • Trucks | 01 |
| • Jeeps & Cars | 93 |
| • Bullet Proof Car | 01 |
| • Vans | 19 |
| • Water Tanker | 01 |

- Interceptor Vehicle 01
- Ambulances 02
- Cranes 03
- Mobile Laboratory 01
- Rapid Intervention Vehicle 01

2. Arms and Ammunition

Have modern arms like AK47, SLR, and CMG to tackle any law & order problem arising out of disaster.

3. Equipments

- Sniffer Dog.
- Gas Cutters.
- Anti-Sabotage Team.
- Search Lights.
- Life Saving Jackets.
- Boat.
- Portable Generators.
- Reflector batons & jackets.
- Boomer Light.

## Functions of Police Department

- Cordoning off the area.
- Establish rescue safe routes.
- Shifting of all vehicles to the parking yards
- Traffic Control.
- Assist in controlling and fighting disaster, salvage operations, rendering first aid and medical health, shifting of affected to rallying post / rescue shelters.
- Identification of the deceased, informing their relatives, removal and disposal of dead bodies.
- Preparing the list of missing persons and to take steps to trace them.
- Maintain law and order.
- Regular patrolling of affected areas.
- Deploy adequate protection at the rescue shelter & at the place of incident for protection of property.

## Traffic Management

- Management of traffic is of paramount importance when disaster takes place.
- 2 NHs & 8 SHs pass through the district. Roads usually witness high density traffic, because of the movement of Mines vehicles, goods vehicles carrying finished steel products, tourist vehicles and Hospet being major exit point.
- There are three traffic stations in the district, headed by the officer of the rank of inspector in Bellary, Hospet & Hampi.
- The staff is well trained, to face any emergency.
- The traffic stations are provided with modern infrastructure, to handle the disasters adequately.

### Parking Places

The following places are identified for parking of vehicles.

- District Stadium, Bellary.
- Open place opposite to BTPS, Kudithini.
- Taluk Stadium, Hospet
- Industrial area, Halakundi.

Apart from the above, the concerned SDPOs will identify other places also for parking of vehicles in their respective sub-divisions.

### Sub Division wise plan

- Bellary Rural, Kudligi & Hospet are the three Sub-Divisions involved in Disaster Management since the major identified industries are situated here.
- Bellary City Sub-Division is also involved, as many Hospitals and other infrastructure available in the city.
- Superintendent of Police will supervise all the operations.
- The four sub-Divisions have 4DSPs, 14 CPI/PIs, 41 PSIs & 1251staff.

### Plan for Kudligi Sub-division

- All 4 Jindal group of companies are situated in the Toranagallu ps.
- On receiving of the information, SDPO will communicate it to the control room, fire tender & health dept.
- In co-ordination with the traffic police of Bellary & Hospet, stop the movement of vehicles towards Toranagallu.

- Alert the hospitals, health centers to be prepared to treat the possible victims of the accident.
- Rush to the spot with maximum possible number of health staff with well equipped ambulances and police staff with arms & ammunition.
- Hospitals are identified to facilitate the free movement of vehicles involved in rescue operation and ensure traffic free roads.
- Parking lots are identified, to park vehicles other than that involved in rescue operations.

**Plan for Bellary Rural Sub-division**

- Monsanto India Limited. Sirivar Village, United Galva Private Limited. Mundargi Industrial Area, (Bellary Rural PS) and Bellary Thermal Power Station, (Kudithini PS) are the industries situated in the sub-division.
- On receiving the information, SDPO will communicate to the Control Room, Fire Tender & Health Dept.
- In co-ordination with the Moka Police Station, Kuditini Police Station & Traffic Police Bellary, stop the movement of vehicles towards Sirivar village, Mundargi Industrial Area & Kuditini.
- Alert the hospitals & health centers, to be prepared to treat the possible victims of the accident.
- Rush to the spot with maximum possible number of health staff with well equipped ambulances and police staff with arms & ammunition.
- Hospitals are identified to facilitate the free movement of vehicles involved in rescue operation and ensure traffic free roads.
- Parking lots are identified, to park vehicles other than that involved in rescue operations.

**Plan for Hospet Sub-division**

- M/s Pampasara Distillery Limited, Hospet. (Chitwadigi PS) is the industry situated in the sub-division.
- On receiving the information, SDPO will communicate to the Control Room, Fire Tender & Health Dept.
- In co-ordination with the traffic police of Hospet, stop the movement of vehicles towards the factory.
- Alert the hospitals & health centers, to be prepared to treat the possible victims of the accident.

- Rush to the spot with maximum possible number of health staff with well equipped ambulances and police staff with arms & ammunition.
- Hospitals are identified to facilitate the free movement of vehicles involved in rescue operation and ensure traffic free roads.
- Parking lots are identified, to park vehicles other than that involved in rescue operations.

# 4

# Animal Behavior

"It is not uncommon for animals to exhibit behavioral changes before an impending disaster. Wild animals often vacate areas, gather in strange groupings and sometimes will even enter into human habitats they normally avoid," animal behavior expert Diana L. Guerrero said. Three days before the earthquake, thousands of toads roamed the streets of Mianzhu, a hard-hit city where at least 2,000 people have been reported killed.

## A pond disappears in Enshi (Hubei province)

In Khao Lak, 50 miles north of Phuket along Thailand's western coast, a dozen elephants giving tourists rides began trumpeting hours before the Dec. 26, 2004 tsunami — about the time the 9.0-magnitude quake fractured the ocean floor. An hour before the wall of waves slammed the resort area, the elephants reportedly again grew agitated and began wailing. Just before disaster struck, they headed for higher ground — some breaking their chains to flee. Flamingos that breed this time of year at Point Calimere sanctuary on India's southern coast left for safer forests well before the tsunami hit, forest officials told the India News. The World Wildlife Fund has attached-satellite collars to some of the elephants that were observed fleeing Patanangala beach in Yala National Park. The WWF announced that it will use the recorded data to track and analyze their movements.

The elephants' trumpeting and erratic behavior is reported to have started at around the time that the earthquake occurred. Could it have been a viable warning? An elephant clears a path in Banda Aceh. Sensitive to ground vibrations, elephants may have detected the undersea quake long before the tsunami hit. The British Press Association reported that an elephant led a group of children to safety after its trainer placed them on its back before the tidal wave crashed ashore. Other pachyderms broke their chains and ran away from the coastlines of Sumatra Island. At the hard-hit Yala National Park in Sri Lanka, stunned wildlife officials reported that hundreds of elephants, leopards, tigers, wild boar, deer, water buffalo, monkeys and smaller mammals and reptiles had escaped unscathed. And while large turtles have been found dead in the debris along the shore of Indonesia's devastated Aceh province, the tsunami's impact on wildlife was "limited," says Frank Momberg, coordinator for emergency response in Aceh for the conservation group Fauna & Flora International.

Tales of animals behaving strangely before the quake and of wildlife escaping to safety have abounded in the wake of the tsunami, raising anew questions about what these members of the animal kingdom knew that humans didn't — and what, if anything, can be learned from it.

Seismologists have sophisticated instruments that can measure quake factors during and after the fact, but experts admit no one can predict exactly when one will happen. Some scientists say certain animals have a kind of sensory hard-wiring that can detect earthquakes ahead of time, which one day might be replicated in man-made instruments.

Reports of animals' "sixth sense" in detecting hurricanes, earthquakes, tsunamis and volcanic eruptions long before the earth starts shaking go back centuries. Rats racing from buildings, sparrows taking flight in flocks, dogs howling incessantly: It's an impressive track record — though anecdotal.

After the Dec. 26 tsunami, a Danish man staying in Ao Sane Beach, north of Phuket, wrote on a Danish Web site: "Dogs are smarter than all of us. . . . [They] started running away up to the hilltops long before we even realized what was coming." Science is iffy on a subject that, for obvious reasons, is difficult to replicate in a laboratory. And there are always explanations and theories that mitigate the mystery of the anecdotes. In the case of this tsunami, says Ken Grant, project coordinator at the Humane Society International Asia office in Bali, Indonesia, a lot of animals escaped simply because they tend to live inland, in the forest. Nevertheless, some scientists are looking for explanations of why some species behave strangely before natural catastrophes, by correlating the animals' sensory abilities with microscopic and invisible sensory stimuli.

Animals' sensory physiology — super-sensitive to sound, temperature, touch, vibration, electrostatic and chemical activity and magnetic fields — gives them a head start in the days and hours before natural calamities. "It appears a lot of animals have sensory organs that detect these micro-tremors and micro-changes that we cannot possibly monitor," says George Pararas-Carayannis, a former University of Hawaii oceanographer and geophysicist who leads the Tsunami Society.

"It's a sensitivity that we humans don't have. But animals through millions of years of evolution have developed it, and that's how they have been able to survive as a species. It is run or perish," says Pararas-Carayannis, author of the 2001 book "The Big One: The Next Great California Earthquake — Why, Where, and When It Will Happen."

Why not humans? When an imminent disaster so unimaginably primal as this occurs, can only creatures in tune with nature at its most elemental sense it coming?

Research shows that many fish are sensitive to low-frequency vibrations and detect tremors long before humans. The bullhead catfish detects magnitude-2 earthquakes so weak people can't feel them at the top of 10-story buildings, says John Caprio, a biological sciences professor at Louisiana State University specializing in fish senses.

An elephant clears a path in Banda Aceh. Sensitive to ground vibrations, elephants may have detected the undersea quake long before the tsunami hit is anecdotal.

Other animals are also extremely sensitive to ground vibrations. Lynette Hart, professor of animal behavior at the University of California-Davis, says that's what probably cued the elephants, which most likely felt the quake in their feet and trunks. Elephants, she says, are known to "lay their trunks on the ground when an airplane or truck generates large seismic noise," as if to feel it.

With the elephant's intelligence — its brain is the largest of terrestrial creatures — "they can figure out what direction the stimulus is coming from, how strong it is, and what evasive action to take," Hart says.

Some animals may have heard the tsunami coming from the moment the quake erupted under the ocean. Species of birds, dogs, elephants, tigers and other animals can detect "infrasound" — frequencies in the range of 1-3 hertz, compared with humans' 100-200-hertz range, says psychobiologist James Walker, director of the Sensory Research Institute at Florida State University. "It's sensitivity to such a low frequency range that most people wouldn't call it sound anymore."

"The Naked Ape" author and animal behavioralist Desmond Morris says cats and dogs are sensitive to sudden electromagnetic changes — like those that precede an earthquake — which is why "many dogs shiver and become scared when a thunderstorm is approaching."

"Canines' sense of smell is 10,000 to 100,000 times superior to that of humans," says Walker, who is starting research to train dogs to detect bladder and prostate cancer in human urine. Dogs' olfactory senses are so sensitive — they're said to be able to smell fear — that it's possible they could pick up on chemical changes in the air before an earthquake.

One dog, who panicked, ran around and barked during the hundreds of aftershocks following the Big Bear Valley California earthquake. Since he had a strong food drive, to change his association, the owner called him as he was running around, asked him if he wanted a bone (distraction), then asked for a behavior (sit) and rewarded him when he responded. Soon he had a good association to aftershocks and quit panicking! The owner could not sleep from all the quake activity so it distracted her as well.

This week, scientists of the Anthropological Survey of India told the Herald Sun of Melbourne, Australia, that members of the ancient tribes it visited on the Andaman and Nicobar islands near the earthquake's epicenter may have been spared because they noticed unusual behavioral changes in the birds, dolphins and lizards.

Chinese researchers have pioneered studies of animals to see how their sensory organs react to minute changes. Their impetus was the earthquake in 1975 that struck the densely populated town of Haicheng in northeast China.

Based largely on sightings of unusual animal behavior, the public was warned and thousands of lives were saved. "A lot of snakes came out of hibernation, and they had a week's notice," says Pararas-Carayannis. Research in China is focused on pigeons, which have shown high sensitivity to ground vibrations in their tibia and fibula nerves, he says. The Chinese are trying to create instruments that replicate such sensitive physiology.

## Sounds Suspicious

There's evidence not all animals pick up on disasters, cautions Ben Hart, Lynette Hart's husband and a UC-Davis professor of animal physiology. His studies have shown that domestic animals' pre-quake behavior is inconsistent. "It is only a few earthquakes that are preceded by unusual behavior," he says. "Most are not, and we don't have the slightest idea why." Ruth Buskirk, a senior lecturer in biological sciences at the University of Texas at Austin, says one reason may be "background noise" — the clutter of sensory stimuli before quakes.

In 1981, Buskirk reviewed the unusual behavior of eels, frogs, snakes, turtles, sea birds, pigeons, chickens, dogs, cats, horses, cows, deer, rats and mice before 36 earthquakes on four continents. She crunched the data every which way.

"Our main conclusion was, boy, the animals can sense anything, including very minor changes that happen before earthquakes, but there's so much background noise during an earthquake" that it's unclear what stimuli the animals are reacting to.

University of Maryland animal behavioralist Ray Stricklin says the reported low wildlife death toll in the tsunami areas may have more to do with chance than cognition. "It is quite possible that animals do have the capacity to sense vibrations more than we humans do, but I don't think it is necessary to attribute to them an ability to recognize there is an earthquake or tsunami threatening and know which way to run."

Bart Houx, an ethologist at Utrecht University in the Netherlands, prefers other explanations than "sensory warning systems" for the low animal casualties — the swimming abilities of certain animals or small animal carcasses being hard to find in the debris.

"I would only be convinced that wild animals had higher survival rates if there are relatively few casualties found in wild coastal territories," he says. "But often these places are very hard to tread, and now, understandably, most people have other things on their mind."

## Reacting to Pressure

In the 12 hours before Hurricane Charley battered Florida's Gulf Coast last year, 14 electronically tagged blacktip sharks off Sarasota bolted into deeper waters.

They stayed away for up to two weeks, then returned. None of them had left its home otherwise in four years of monitoring, according to scientists at Mote Marine Laboratory in Sarasota.

The sharks did the same thing three years earlier when Tropical Storm Gabrielle hit.

"I think these animals are more attuned to their environment than we give them credit for," says Michelle Heupel, a staff scientist. "When things change, they may not understand why it's happening, but the change itself may trigger some instinct to move to an area that is safer for them." Heupel says what coincided with the sharks' abrupt flight was a big drop in barometric pressure. "Not that they thought, 'Oh my God, the pressure's changing and we've got to go,' "she says. "We know so little about how animals sense these things. These findings are just a glimpse into what animals are doing when we're not looking."

## Animals sensed tsunami much in advance

By Chennai Online News Service

Cuddalore/Keezhputhupattu, Dec 31: Five days after the tsunami wrecked villages across the coastal regions of India, the officials are realising that the number of dead animals - cattle, goat and dogs - in the killer waves is much fewer than perhaps seen in calamities such as cyclones and floods.

"Villagers in this part do not tie their animals. This may have helped them to run away before the waves hit the villages," said an official overseeing the relief work in Cuddalore district.

An interesting theory that is emerging is that the animals sensed the tsunami much in advance and it helped them to run away to safer places. "My three dogs were barking and howling with no reason at around 7 a.m. on Sunday. I asked them to keep quiet but they continued barking and were restless," said Fr P A Sampath Kumar of Holy Family Church at Keezhputhupattu, about 15 km from Pondicherry.

The first waves of the killer tsunami hit Keezhputhupattu at about 8.30 a.m. which was followed by another at 9 a.m. ravaging this fishing village. "I definitely think that my dogs sensed the tsunami," the priest said. (Agencies)

Johannesburg, December 30: Wild animals seem to have escaped the Indian Ocean tsunami, adding weight to notions they possess a "sixth sense" for disasters, experts said on Thursday.

Sri Lankan wildlife officials have said the giant waves that killed over 24,000 people along the Indian Ocean island's coast seemingly missed wild beasts, with no dead animals found.

"No elephants are dead, not even a dead hare or rabbit. I think animals can sense disaster. They have a sixth sense. They know when things are happening," H.D. Ratnayake, Deputy Director of Sri Lanka's Wildlife Department, said on Wednesday.

The waves washed floodwaters up to 3 km (2 miles) inland at Yala National Park in the ravaged southeast, Sri Lanka's biggest wildlife reserve and home to hundreds of wild elephants and several leopards. "There has been a lot of anecdotal evidence about dogs barking or birds migrating before volcanic eruptions or earthquakes. But it has not been proven," said Matthew van Lierop, an animal behaviour specialist at Johannesburg Zoo.

**Cats:** Cats will be jumpy. You may see warning signs such as hiding, running around frantically trying to escape to the outside, hanging on screens and meowing, or behavior unusual for your pet. Many times they will be aggressive, or will want to stick close to or be on top of you. Pacing, hissing, or growling can also be symptoms. Most cats will hide, so check their favorite hiding places and behind cupboards, refrigerators, sofas, beds, in closets, in the backs of washers and dryers, and on top of cupboards, shelves and behind the water heater. Check small spaces in the backs of any appliance since they will often seek out dark and small areas.

**Horses and Livestock:** Hoofed animals often refuse to enter their barns or pens and often refuse to tie. They tend to group together in open areas, act nervous, or pace.

**Other Animals:** Caged birds will often hang on their cage, sometimes they will flap frantically, or they can be abnormally quiet. Breeding birds will often abandon their eggs or discard them from the nest. Other animals will exhibit abnormal behavior. Some of the unusual changes are that; Hibernating animal swill emerge early (snakes, bears, etc.); Spiders and ants will move indoors; Rodents will invade the house or if they are in residence will disappear; Wild birds become quiet or are not visible; Remember these are only clues that something may be wrong.

**Dogs:** Dogs will usually not hide. Behavior exhibited before quake activity includes howling, whining, barking, restlessness, aggression, and increased devotion to owners. They will usually run around, and can bolt through gates, windows, or doors, or stick to you like glue. Some dogs will become more protective or aggressive while others will be fearful or act dejected. Pay attention to their personalities and individual needs and you will be able to avoid trouble. Drastic differences in the number of advertised lost dogs and the animal shelter loads can precede quake activity in a specific area. Large increases in these numbers could give you a clue to up coming earth activity.

Is there any reason to think we could use animals as a way to alert to natural disasters?

However the technique for identifying precursory behavior would have to bere fined.

Earlier this year the Washington Times reported that the Chinese will again use animals as seismic sentries. There is also a geologist in Northern California who collects reports of unusual animal behavior in an attempt to correlate behavior changes to seismic activity.

## China uses animals to monitor Earthquakes

Beijing, China, Jul. 31 (UPI) — In a throwback to the last days of Maoism, a city in northeast China said Saturday it will again use animal observation as a means of earthquake prediction.

The birds, like the albatross, can be greatly affected by changes in the weather. So can they predict when the next storm will hit? Seagulls are sensitive to barometric changes. It's thought that they return to land if they feel pressure drop.

# 5

# Livestock Management During Natural Disasters

A disaster (from Latin meaning, "bad star') is the impact of a natural or man-made event that negatively affects life, property, livelihood or industry often resulting in permanent changes to human societies, ecosystems and environment. The event itself is not a disaster; it is the impact that is a disaster. Their possibility of occurrence, time, place and severity of the strike can be reasonably and in some cases accurately predicted by technological and scientific advances. Hence, we can to some extent reduce the impact of damage though we cannot reduce the extent of damage itself. Despite the severe impacts suffered – including trauma, starvation, dehydration, infection, disease and shock-animals are often the silent victims of disasters, and there is a real need around for the provision of effective training and management programmes to ensure that their survival and welfare are adequately accounted for. This demands the study of disaster management in methodical and orderly approach.

The World Health Organization (WHO) defines a 'disaster' as any occurrence that causes damage, destruction, ecological disruption, loss of human life, human suffering, deterioration of health and health services on a scale sufficient to warrant an extraordinary response from outside the affected community or area (WHO, 1999). It is an event, concentrated in time and space, which causes social, economic, cultural and political devastation and which affects both individual people and communities (Kumar, 1998).

**Classification of Disasters:** Disasters can be classified by nature, timing, predictability and type of impact (Thapliyal, 2003).

**Table 1** Disasters according to timing and predictability

| Slow | Quick | |
|---|---|---|
| | **Predictable** | **Unpredictable/Sudden** |
| Drought | Cyclone | Earthquake |
| Famine | Flood | Landslide |
| Food shortage | Typhoon | Avalanche |

## Scenario of natural disaster management in India

In India, relief often does not reach to the affected areas until quite late, usually between 24 and 72 hours after the disaster has struck. It is not always professionally organized (Bandyopadhyay, 1999). Protecting and saving human life is the first priority in disaster relief and protecting property (which includes animals) is the second. Due to absence of preparedness for disasters and lack of awareness there is high mortality of livestock. It is the affected people themselves who must be the first to respond to the disaster, they must guide and take care of themselves until outside relief arrives. It is essential to have a well designed and practical disaster management plan for livestock.

**Severity indices (SI) for disasters in India:** Disasters in India can be categorized into four types-

| | | |
|---|---|---|
| Group I (SI = 10) | : | Floods & Earthquakes |
| Group II (SI= 8-10) | : | Cyclones, Drought, |
| Group III (SI= 6-8) | : | Forest fires, Epidemics, Thunderstorm, Hailstorm Lightning, Tornado, Landslides etc. |
| Group IV (SI=<6) | : | Dust Storms, Heat & Cold Waves |

**Strategies for Management of Livestock in Disaster Prone Areas**

When animals are affected by disaster, the main problems are (Sen and Chander, 2003) spoilage of food and/or the water supply, zoonoses, animal bites, emotional involvement of the owners with the animals, reduced dairy and livestock production, due to the scarcity of feed and water, high livestock mortality rates and damage to both domestic and wild animal species, due to lack of feed and water, physical injury and the diseases which spread during and after a disaster.

**Basic rules for animal protection during disasters**

1. Veterinarians and animal protection experts should be included in disaster assessment teams and their advice used in community disaster planning.
2. Where possible, humanitarian relief bodies and local governments should involve animal care groups such as international animal welfare relief

NGOs like International working group on animals in disasters (IWGAID) to provide shelter, rescue and veterinary care and generally augment the humanitarian community.

3. Humanitarian aid workers should be given basic stray animal awareness training for safety reasons.
4. Joint training between animal care and humanitarian relief workers will enhance the ability of both communities to work together and ensure an approach to disaster management that saves both people and animals at the least cost.
5. Policy makers should take into account practical indigenous techniques and economic, trade or social restrictions.

**Housing management**

1. Animals should not be kept under direct sunlight; they should be kept under shade of trees.
2. No over crowding of animal in shed should be there.
3. Iron sheet roof should also be covered with thatch or asbestos sheet.
4. Upper layer of Kachha floor should be replaced with new sand at every six Months interval, so that load of organism can be reduced.
5. Spots closer to temples, churches, masjids are generally ideal for temporary drought relief camp.

**Feeding management**

1. Provide essential nutrients to maintain the physiological function and to protect productive traits.
2. Application of fodder conservation techniques.
3. Management of good stocking rates in pasture land.
4. Grow drought-resistant plants and rear drought resistant livestock species/ strain.
5. Conservation of farming practices.
6. Animals should be allowed to graze & feed only in early morning or late evening.

**Water management during scarcity**

1. Watering every other day could reduce WI by 25% without ill effect.
2. Lactating and pregnant animal be given priority over young and bullock.
3. Crossbred over local breeds, sick animal over healthy.
4. Precaution to avoid wastage of water.
5. Salt intake of the animal should be restricted.

6. Water should be mixed with ‘Gur/jaggery as it satisfy the thirst.
7. Provide water to animals in small quantity and more frequently.
8. Water conservation during the rainy season (dams and ponds).

## Caring for livestock during disaster

When dealing with livestock during emergencies, it is critical to reestablish your priorities. The first priority should be your personal safety and welfare, followed by the safety and welfare of other people, and finally animals and property. If you are safe, you can do more to benefit animals. If you are at risk, so is their welfare and health. Follow official instructions for access and safety when reentering a disaster zone. The first logical step in caring for livestock and other animals is to locate, control and provide for those animals. Locating animals often is limitedby transportation blockages from the disaster because normal routes may not beavailable. If the emergency manager is difficult tofind, contact local law enforcement for information. In a disasterarea affected by earthquake and cyclone, remember hazards may still occur, including downed power lines, flooded areas, unstable roads and highways, gas and utility leaks, debris and wreckage, vandals and looters.

### Sensitivity

Often violent impacts of disaster disorient and temporarily alter the behavioral state of livestock. When, and if, you locate your animals, realize that they may be upset, confused and agitated. They need help finding their normal behavioral pattern. Here are some proven techniques for doing this:

1. Handle livestock quietly, calmly and in a manner they are familiar.
2. Wear clothing and use vehicles that are familiar to them.
3. If possible, keep or reunite familiar animal groups with each other.
4. As soon as possible, place them in familiar settings or one which is quiet, calm and insulated from additional stimuli.
5. Soft music and familiar sounds may help calm livestock.
6. If possible, clean the animals (i.e., wipe out their eyes, mouths and nostrils).
7. If possible, move animals away from the residue of the disaster.
8. Treat wounds of injured animals so their comfort level improves.

### Feed, safety and shelter

The shortage of livestock feeding is caused by floods and droughts and there is no single year in the Indian history ‘in which the floods have not occurred in one part of the country and the droughts in the other. The scarcity of animal feed caused by floods is of a temporary, nature. During the droughts, however severe shortage of animal feed especially roughages is encountered. This has an adverse effect on feed resources as dried roughages alone account for over 50 to 80 per cent of supply of dry matter and TDN required for ruminants viz., sheep, cattle and goats. Failure of monsoon is the main factor responsible for droughts in Asia. While co-efficient of variation in monsoon rainfall for the Indian subcontinent is only 10 per cent, the same for Gujarat, Maharashtra, Karnataka, Andhra Pradesh and Rajasthan is over 35 per cent. In parts of Rajasthan, Gujarat. Saurashtra and some districts of the Deccan Plateau it ranges from 50 per cent to 100 per cent. Certain areas are, therefore, more prone for fodder scarcity than others. Incidentally, these areas make a major contribution towards production of oilseeds and coarse grains. The shortage of these crops aggravates the supply of oil cakes and straws. Perennial irrigation system has been developed in such areas through construction of dams and canals.

However, redeeming feature in supply of livestock feed is that the commercial crops continue to be cultivated in selected pockets with ensured irrigation even in the worst drought affected zones. The use of products of such commercial crops, drought resistant vegetations, in combination with NPN source of protein and by-products of sugarcane industry, molasses as source of energy could be used for meeting the immediate nutritional requirements under conditions of scarcity. Certain varieties of tree leaves and cakes of inedible oilseeds could be used to meet the essential requirements of intact protein in ruminants. This strategy was successfully applied in the State of Maharashtra in India during droughts of 1972-73. The cattle relief camps were set up around the sugarcane factories located in the drought affected zones. Large scale feeding of bagasse, molasses in combination with urea and mineral supplements was adopted. The feed formulations developed through experimentation were tried on large population of cattle without any detrimental effects.

Animals and livestock often relate security to the familiarity of their surroundings. In some cases, you may be able to return them to familiarsurroundings and enhance their recovery. Unfortunately, a disaster often impactsthe familiar surroundings altering the landscape's character, feel, smell, look andlayout. To enhance the animal's comfort level, find another place with similarcharacteristics. Move the livestock there until you can remedy the damage.Feed and water are a big part in livestock disaster recovery. In additionto the health and nutrient aspects of appropriate feed and water, livestock canbecome very picky to eat and drink if their feed and water do not smell and tastefamiliar. This nervousness is usually greater during and after disasters. A calm and quiet shelter serves both physical and emotional needs for livestock.

**Proper animal evacuation policy rules**

1. Even with proper early warning, adequate resources must be available to evacuate animals, otherwise they may die or be stolen — a major loss to a fragile economy and a foundation for future conflict.
2. Sanitation and safety considerations restrict animals from camps yet disaster victims know their animals are their future and may refuse to enter camps without animals being provided for.
3. Whenever practical, areas adjacent to camps should be provided, perhaps maintained by the victims with help from animal care professionals.
4. While disaster victims should have the right to keep their animals, the introduction of new animals in a host community can be very damaging to the local economy, so a balanced policy is needed.
5. Animal welfare professionals should co-design with the humanitarian community policies and procedures to reduce losses from evacuations.

## Disease prevention and control

Large scale disease outbreaks are among the most serious of disasters, having the potential to kill millions of animals and people and to devastate the economies of local communities and entire countries. Epizootics can spread quickly across political boundaries and threaten the global livestock and poultry industries. Veterinarians, veterinary servicesand other animalhealth and welfare professionals can reduce these risksin many practical ways. These include the provisionof advice on basic health and hygiene requirementsfor livestock management and movement. Organizing"train the trainer" programs is a useful means oftransferring knowledge from trained professionals toother people working within communities. Even inthe face of a disaster, it is important to try and maintaindisease preventionand controlprogramsalreadyestablishedand to providea basis for these to beadjustedto deal with the disaster event.

Where slaughter of infected and at risk animals is a necessary part of controlling a disease, it should be carried out as humanely as possible, and in compliance with OIE standards. Vaccination programs to control certain diseases, supervised by the Official Veterinary Service, can also have a significant effect in preventing the introduction and spread of these diseases.

## Proper carcass disposal

1. By burning - For large animal 4m diameter and 1m tall pit should be made.

   Cross trench pit method: normally a gallon of kerosene or old rubber tyres can also be used. Surface burning: when there is scarcity of labour or paucity of time this can be used.

2. By burying - A deep pit usually 8-9 feet should be made. Use of quick lime, common salt and other disinfectant may be used in these pits.

## Difficulties

1. **Animal reactions when under duress:** Animals can be resistant in disasters that are annoying, but not frightening, suchas blizzards and slow floods. During disasters, animalownersmay see a behavioral pattern fromtheirlivestock that they are both unpreparedandunable to handle.
2. **Access and transportation difficulties:** Animal evacuation from a disaster area must occur in a coordinated manner under the direction of the incident command team to allow success without impeding handling of the disaster and while protecting public safety.
3. **Equipment and facility design risks:** Having properly designed and effectively maintained equipment and facilities are critical during disasters.
4. **Losing focus on the disaster event:** Although it's not desirable for livestock owners to face so many disasters that they also develop this broad focus, there is one key approach that helps enhance safety in tense situations—teamwork.

**Community participation in animal disaster management**

In India, relief often does not reach affected areas until quite late on, usually between 24 and 72 hours after the disaster has struck. In most cases, this is because of communication problems and because the relief teams do not have the capacity to get there by any quicker means. Furthermore, the relief operations are not always professionally organized (2). Therefore, it is the affected people themselves who must be the first to respond to the disaster; they must guide and take care of themselves until outside relief arrives. Even after a disaster they play a major role in facilitating that relief.

In regions where natural disasters are a common occurrence, the community usually has some inbuilt socio-cultural systems to deal with them. For example, through the ages, the Somali pastoralists have developed effective survival mechanisms to mitigate the impact of droughts and increase the chances of their own survival and that of their livestock. For example, they rear two or more species of livestock as a buffer against the loss of animals in drought, and members of the clan who can afford it offer animals to the less fortunate members. In developing countries, local resources and expertise, which can identify common hazards and prioritise mitigation and planning strategies to reduce the impact of disasters, need to be integrated with government initiatives. One programme which takes this approach of involving the local community in disaster preparedness is the Community-based Disaster Preparedness programme.

This programme aims to strengthen the capacity of local communities to cope with emergencies arising from sudden natural or man-made disasters, by mobilizing all the local and external resources that are available. Development issues in India have traditionally followed a top down approach without much consideration of local demands and sensitivities. Community involvement in development programmes is an area that is usually neglected. However, local government, or Panchayati Raj Institutions (PRIs), have a vital part to play in disaster management and their role must not be ignored, as without an effective local government relief agency, proper disaster management, community based or top-down, is impossible. Community based relief requires an effective local government relief agency that initiates, facilitates, encourages, monitors and matches the local community-based efforts. When disasters occur, it is local governments that are in the best position to provide leadership, supervise the distribution of relief goods and medicine, manage evacuations and provide equipment and tools. They can also play a significant role in long-term risk reduction. Recognizing the importance of community involvement in disaster management, a community based disaster management programme is being implemented in Orissa by the Orissa State Disaster Mitigation Authority.

Block level PRIs (for administrative purposes each district in India is divided into blocks which contain several villages; there are usually nine or ten blocks in a district) are the agencies through which the project is being implemented, with the aim of establishing a disaster management plan practical enough to minimize the impact of disasters and to educate the local community in disaster management practices.

## Government Responsibilities

The main responsibility for disaster relief lies with the state governments, and the Government of India supplements the efforts of the state governments by offering logistic and financial support. As per the recommendations of the Eleventh Finance Commission, two schemes, namely, the Calamity Relief Fund (CRF) scheme and the National Calamity Contingency Fund (NCCF) scheme have been established for the period 2000-2001 to 2004-2005. Both these funds are available for meeting the cost of providing immediate relief to the victims of natural disasters. Each state has a CRF, and when disaster occurs 75% of the total budget for disaster management is provided by the central government and the remaining 25% by the state government. The NCCF provides assistance to the states in the event of severe natural calamities where the expenditure on relief exceeds the prescribed norms and cannot be met by the existing funds in the CRF of the state concerned.

The state governments have a state cabinet and a state Crisis Management Group (CMG), headed by a chief secretary. Figure 1 shows the national mechanism for responding to natural disasters. Various government agencies play different roles in disaster management as presented in Table X. When disasters occur, the armed forces, under the Ministry of Defence, and the central Para-military forces, under the Ministry of Home Affairs, are deployed for emergency rescue work in the affected areas. A national body called the National Committee on Disaster Management was recently established under the Chairmanship of the Prime Minister, with representatives from all political parties at both national and state level. Its purpose is inter alia to suggest what institutional and legislative measures should be included in an effective and long-term strategy for dealing with major natural calamities in the future. Furthermore, a High Powered Committee (HPC) was established in August 1999 to prepare comprehensive model plans for the management of disasters at National, State and District levels. The National Committee on Disaster Management and the HPC has recognized the importance of the involvement of the PRIs in disaster management. At village, district, and block levels, committees should monitor relief work. Ideally, as suggested by the EMI, the main responsibility of disaster relief should lie with local government and the state government should monitor their work and provide financial support. The central government should provide training, information on the latest disaster mitigation measures, financial assistance, subsidies, guidance, and co-ordinate the services for disaster response and recovery activities.

## Voluntary Agencies and Organizations

Disasters can overstretch the emergency resources of local, state and central governments and when this happens the value of additional support from voluntary agencies has been demonstrated time and again in different countries. One method of involving voluntary agencies in the planning for disasters is to group them, where appropriate, on the basis of their mandate and link them to the statutory authorities responsible for those functions. This functional grouping can clarify the contributions which individual voluntary organisations can make and enable the statutory authorities and voluntary organisations to make the most of the voluntary contribution.

## Role of Veterinarians in Disaster

During disasters, the role of veterinarians is to ensure high standards of animal health and to reduce mortality among animals. Veterinarians can play a major role in promoting local pre-disaster planning at community level, which places a high priority on facilitating livestock and pet evacuation. Heath suggests that an 'all hazards' approach would facilitate the integration of veterinarians into disaster management efforts. This approach is based on the concept that regardless of the impact of different types of disasters, the socio-economic consequences, including the economic impact on animal agriculture, are similar. Veterinarians have a role to play in all stages of disaster mitigation and management, but it is during relief efforts that they can play a crucial role in increasing the survivability of animals that are victims, and of those that are deployed in rescue teams. The contribution of veterinarians will be most effective if they integrate their expertise with other local, national and international groups and agencies involved in disaster management.

Preparing a disaster box for livestock has great merit. Consider keeping this type of box in your vehicle or tack compartment of your trailer, if you have one. Recommended items for a livestock disaster box include:

Tack, ropes, halters

Concentrated feed, hay, supplements and medicines

Copies of ownership papers

Buckets or feed nets

Garden hose

Flashlight or lantern

Blankets or tarps

Lights, portable radio and spare batteries

Livestock first aid supplies

**Phases of disaster management (FEMA, 1998)**

Basic components of any disaster management plan consists of following four steps: Mitigation, Preparedness, Response and Recovery.

| Phase | Action |
|---|---|
| **Mitigation**<br>Preventing future emergencies or minimising their effects | Includes any activities that prevent an emergency , reduce the chances of an emergency happening , or reduce the damaging effects of unavoidable emergencies , e.g. buying flood & fire insurance for homes mitigation activities take place before & after emergencies |
| **Preparedness**<br>Preparing to handle an emergency | Includes plans or preparations made to save lives & to help response &rescue operations ,<br>Eg evacuation plans & stocking food & water<br>Preparedness activities take place before an emergency occurs |
| **Response**<br>Responding safely to an emergency | Includes action taken to save lives &prevent further property damage in an emergency situation. Response is putting preparedness plans into action, E.g. seeking shelter from a tornado or turning off gas valves in an earthquake<br>Response activities take place during an emergency |
| **Recovery**<br>Recovering from an emergency | Includes action taken to a normal or an even safer situation following an emergency ,<br>e.g. getting financial assistance to help pay for the repairs<br>Response activities take place after an emergency |

i. **Mitigation (**Preventing future emergencies or minimizing their effects)

Includes any activities that prevent an emergency, reduce the chances of an emergency happening, or reduce the damaging effects of unavoidable emergencies, e.g. buying earthquake and cyclone insurance for homes. Mitigation activities take place before and after emergencies.

ii. **Preparedness** (Preparing to handle an emergency)

Includes plans or preparations made to save lives and to help response and rescue operations e.g. evacuation plans and stocking food and water. Preparedness activities take place before an emergency occurs. Mitigation and preparedness measures go hand in hand for vulnerability reduction and rapid professional response to disasters.

iii. **Response** (Responding safely to an emergency) includes actions taken to save lives and prevent further property damage in an emergency situation. Response is putting preparedness plans into action, e.g. seeking shelter from a tornado or turning off gas valves in an earthquake. Response activities take place during an emergency.

iv. **Recovery** (Recovering from an emergency) Includes actions taken to return to a normal or an even safer situation following an emergency, e.g. getting financial assistance to help pay for the repairs. Recovery activities take place after an emergency. Proper care and treatment, deworming and vaccination of animals in affected areas are to be carried out on priority basis in affected areas.

# Conclusion

In developing countries, like India, disasters are a common phenomenon every year. The most badly affected are the poor and marginalized communities in India, who suffer most in terms of human and property loss when disaster strikes. Not only are they the worst hit, but also, their capacity to recover from disaster is limited by the social, economic and political conditions in which they live. In many developing countries the institutional mechanisms for facing disaster are not sufficient to meet the challenge. This results in the severe loss of human and livestock life which could be saved, to a greater or lesser extent, if preparedness, response and recovery mechanisms were in order. In terms of disaster preparedness, developing countries are well behind the developed nations. Protecting and saving human life is the first priority in disaster relief and protecting property (which includes animals) is the second. Because of this, emergency management officials in India are not trained to deal with animals or to restore animal related business. This is something that requires more attention from the National Crisis Management Committee and the state CMGs, and livestock relief after natural disasters needs to be given greater emphasis. The disaster-prone states of India should also develop disaster mitigation and management plans for livestock. Experience has shown that disaster management to date has been reactionary rather than proactive and preventative. Livestock relief plans should be developed as a part of preparedness activities and not during a natural disaster. Disaster management should be integrated with long-term development planning, and a holistic approach, rather than a segmented approach, should be taken, with popular participation involving local communities. Development and disaster management planning should go hand-in-hand and development models must have in-built components for disaster reduction, mitigation and preparedness.

# References

Anonymous. Glossary of Meteorology (June 2000). "Cyclonic circulation"

Bandyopadhyay S.K. 1999. Food and Agricultural Organization of the United Nations (FAO) Mission Report on Agricultural Rehabilitation of Cyclone Affected Areas of Orissa. FAO, Rome (http://www.un.org.in/dmt/orissa/FAOrprt.htm).

Bhanja S.K., Mohanty P.K., Sahoo A. and Patra R.C. 1999. Impact of supercyclone in Orissa on livestock wealth and its remedial measures: a report. Indian Veterinary Research Institute, Izatnagar, India, 25 pp.

Bhanutej N., Jathar D., Panicker A., Tiwari D. and Uprety A. (2002). Prayers from a parched land. In The Week, 4 August. Malayala Manorama Publications, Kochi, Kerala, India (http://www.the-week.com/22aug04/events11.htm).

Datta, D. 1998. Damage due to severe tropical cyclone in Northwest India. Newsletter. INCEDE. International Center for Disaster-Mitigation Engineering, Institute of Industrial Science, University of Tokyo, 7 (2):5–6 (http://incede.iis.utokyo.ac.jp/Newsletter/7.2/7-2-2.htm).

Disaster Management in India. 2004. National Disaster Management Division, Ministry of Home Affairs, Government of India. (http://www.ndmindia.nic.in/EQProjects/Disaster%20Management%20in%20India%20-%20A%20Status%20Report%20-%20August%202004.pdf)

Federal Emergency Management Agency (FEMA) (1998). Animals in disaster – module A: awareness and preparedness. Emergency Management Institute (EMI) independent study course. EMI, Emmitsburg, Maryland (www.training.fema.gov/EMIWeb/is10.htm).

Government of India (GOI) (2000). Contingency Plan – Drought 2000. Department of Agriculture and Cooperation, Ministry of Agriculture, GOI, New Delhi (http://www.ndmindia.nic.in/documents/contplan_drot2000. html).

Government of India (GOI) (2002). Annual Report 2001– 2002. Department of Agriculture and Cooperation, Ministry of Agriculture, GOI, New Delhi.

Government of India (GOI) (2002). Annual Report 2001–2002. Department of Agriculture and Cooperation, Ministry of Agriculture, GOI, New Delhi.

Government of India (GOI). 2002. Agricultural statistics at a glance. Department of Agriculture and Cooperation, Ministry of Agriculture, GOI, New Delhi.

Government of India (GOI). 2002. Annual Report 2001–2002. Department of Agriculture and Cooperation, Ministry of Agriculture, GOI, New Delhi. (http://en.wikipedia.org/wiki/American_Meteorological_Society)

Gupta HK. 2003. Disaster Management. Indian National Science Academy.Orient Blackswan.

Hodgkinson PE and Stewart M. 1991.Coping with Catastrophe: A Handbook of Disaster Management.Routledge. Sharma VK. 2001. Disaster Management. National Centre for Disaster Management, India.

http://en.wikipedia.org/wiki/Calcification

http://en.wikipedia.org/wiki/Chongqing,_China

http://en.wikipedia.org/wiki/Community_emergency_response_team\

http://en.wikipedia.org/wiki/Cruise_ships

http://en.wikipedia.org/wiki International_Federation_of_Red_Cross_and_Red_ Crescent_ Societies

https://www.worldenergy.org/data/resources/resource/coal/ (ACCESSWD ON 13-09-2017)

http://www.arkanimals.com/dlg/seismic_sentries_animal_disaster_predictions.htm

http://www.washtimes.com/upi-breaking/20040731-012717-9883r.htm

http://www.boingboing.net/2010/01/26/science-question-fro-5.html

http://www.ndma.gov.in/en/media-public-awareness/disaster/man-made-disaster/biological.html. Source: National Disaster Management Authority, Government of India.

Jain S.K., Singh R.P., Gupta V.K. and Nagar A. 1992. Garhwal Earthquake of Oct. 20, 1991. The Earthquake Engineering Research Institute (EERI) special earthquake report.

Kasindorf M., McMahon P., Watson T. and Sharp D. (2002). Drought likely to spare U.S. economy as a whole. USA Today, 25 August (http://www.usatoday.com/news/nation/2002-08-25-drought_x.htm).

Keim, M. E. 2006. Cyclones, Tsunamis, and Human Health: The Key Role of Preparedness. Oceanography 19(2): 40–49.

Mileti D. S. 1999. Disasters by design. Washington, DC: Joseph Henry Press.

National Drought Mitigation Center (NDMC) (2002). What is drought? Understandingand defining drought. National Drought Mitigation Center, University of Nebraska, Lincoln (http://www.drought.unl.edu/whatis/concept).

Sen, A. and Chander, M. 2003. Disaster management in India: the case of livestock and poultry. Rev. Sci. Tech. Off. Int. Epiz., 22 (3):915–930.

Shultz, J. M. Russell, J. and Espinel Z. 2005. Epidemiology of Tropical Cyclones: The Dynamics of Disaster, Disease, and Development Forecasting. Epidemiol Rev; 27:21–35.

Siddique, A.K. and Eusok, A. 1987. Cyclone deaths in Bangladesh, May 1985: who was at risk? Trop Geogr Med 39:3–8.

Swami S.K. (2001). Management of drought in India. In Proc. UNDP Sub-Regional Seminar on Drought Mitigation, 28–29 August, Tehran (http://www.ndmindia.nic.in/documents/document.html).

Thapliyal, B. K. 2003. Training module on planning for disaster preparedness and mitigation. A handbook for trainers on participatory local development. Food and Agriculture Organization of the United Nations, FAO Regional Office for Asia and the Pacific Bangkok, Thailand pp: 79–83.

Thomalla, F. and Schmuck, H. 2004. "We all knew the disaster was coming": disaster preparedness and the cyclone of 1999 in Orissa, India. Disasters 28:373–87.

United States Department of Agriculture (2002). Drought Information website (http://drought.fsa.usda.gov).

WHO, (World Health Organization), (1999). Community Emergency Preparedness: A Manual for Managers and Policy-makers, Received March 28, 2005. (http://whqlibdoc.who.int/publications/9241545194.pdf

FSC
www.fsc.org
MIX
Papier | Fördert gute Waldnutzung
FSC® C083411

Kolibri 360 GmbH
Ferdinand-Jühlke-Straße 7
99095 Erfurt, Deutschland
produktsicherheit@kolibri360.de